Sunlight on the Grass:
A Student Guide to the
AQA GCSE
Short Story Anthology

Table of Contents

Introduction

If you have bought this book you are likely to be studying AQA GCSE. *Sunlight on the Grass* is an anthology of seven short stories chosen by the exam board for students to study. We wrote this book because there was nothing else in print that dealt specifically with this important part of the specification. We hope you find the notes and analysis of each story helpful as well as the model answers which follow them. We also hope that reading this guide will help you understand and appreciate the stories better and give you ways to think about them and to write about them, but remember there is no substitute for knowing the stories very well yourself. You may disagree with some of our ideas about the stories, but that is good because it shows that you are developing your own ideas and becoming an independent reader.

How you are studying these stories and how you will be assessed about your study of them depends on the decisions made by your teacher about the specification and it also depends on which specification you are being entered for. We summarize the possibilities below:

English Literature 4710

If you are studying this anthology for AQA English Literature GCSE, then it is an optional set text for Unit 1 which is called 'Exploring Modern Texts'. The exam paper is ninety minutes long and in that hour and a half you answer two questions: you will be studying another set text for this paper as well as the anthology. You are allowed copies of the anthology in the exam room to consult and you have a choice of two questions on each of your two set texts. In other words, you have 45 minutes to write an answer to the question you choose to do on *Sunlight on the Grass*. Examples of the questions that the exam board has set are discussed and answered in the section entitled Model Essays: you have to write about two of the seven stories, but you do not have to compare or contrast then in any way – that is not part of the assessment. Essentially, therefore, if you allow time for planning and thinking about the question and your response to it, you have about twenty minutes to write on each story in the examination.

In the English Literature exam, as we are sure your teachers have told you, your work is being assessed against two separate assessment objectives (often called AOs). There are, in fact, four assessment objectives for English Literature, but only the first two are assessed on this exam paper.

Assessment Objective 1 requires you to:

respond to texts critically and imaginatively; select and evaluate textual detail to illustrate and support interpretations.

To address this assessment objective successfully, you need to show that you are aware that stories can be interpreted differently and you need to have a clear sense of how **you** respond critically to each story – Do you like it? Why? What is its overall effect? What is its tone, mood and atmosphere? You also need to refer to the text – "select... textual detail" – by using quotations and you have to "evaluate" the textual detail you select. In practice this means that every time you use a quotation, you should write a sentence after it which evaluates it – which explains why it is important or what its effect is. We would also advise you to keep your quotations as short and pithy as possible: after all, you have the text with you in the exam and you get no marks for copying out long parts of the story. And you have limited time – twenty minutes on each story, so you have to think and write quickly and effectively.

Assessment objective 2 requires you to:

explain how language, structure and form contribute to writers' presentation of ideas, themes and settings.

We are sure that you will have a good grasp of each story's themes, but note that this assessment objective asks you to focus on the ways language, form and structure contribute to the ways in which the ideas, themes and settings are brought out in the stories. You might feel a little puzzled about how to write about structure in a short story. (In poetry, by contrast, there is often a readily identifiable structure involving a rhyme scheme and stanzas or line length), but short stories also use structure, so elements like how a story begins and ends is a question of structure; flashbacks and changes of tense are part of structure; the order of events and the way writers choose to reveal some information slowly are parts of structure. Form too might be a question of when a writer reveals something to the reader – a piece of information that provides a twist or unexpected ending to the story.

English Language 4705

You might be using *Sunlight on Grass* for the Controlled Assessment of Unit 3 which is called Understanding Spoken and Written Texts and Writing Creatively. The whole anthology would count as an extended text for Part A of this unit.

English 4700

If you are studying for this specification, then *Sunlight on the Grass* is an optional text for the Controlled Assessment of Unit 3 which is called Understanding and Producing Creative Texts. However, for this unit there is a requirement to study texts from a Different Culture, so only three of the stories in the anthology could be used: 'Anil', 'Something Old, Something New' and 'On Seeing the 100% Perfect Girl One Beautiful April Morning'.

Whichever specification you are using, we are sure you will find this guide useful.

'My Polish Teacher's Tie' – Helen Dunmore

Author

Helen Dunmore was born in 1952 in Yorkshire. She was the second of four children and her father was the eldest of twelve; she attributes being part of a large family as instrumental to her prolific writing career. Amongst her various credentials she won the inaugural Orange Prize for Fiction in 1996, a prize awarded specifically to female writers, with her third novel *A Spell of Winter*.

'My Polish Teacher's Tie' is one of 18 short stories extracted from her book *Ice Cream. Ice Cream* was also nominated for the Orange Prize in 2003.

The author's recurrent themes consist of love and loss, food and landscapes.

Plot

'My Polish Teacher's Tie' is set in a school canteen and its protagonist (the leading character) is a school dinner lady, Carla Carter. It is written in the first person. In the fourth paragraph Carla reveals that she is half Polish, although she does not speak the language. Her English father objected to Carla speaking Polish with her mother, believing that it would confuse his child.

At the weekly staff meeting the Head announces plans to arrange a teacher exchange. We are told that several Polish teachers are looking for pen friends in English schools (to improve their written English). Carla volunteers and begins corresponding with Stefan, or Steve as he prefers to be known. Carla harbours a nagging guilt, knowing that Steve believes he is communicating with another teacher, not a school dinner lady.

Through their correspondence Carla's love of poetry is rekindled and her hunger to learn more of her Polish heritage exposed. Steve's letters provide her with a great source of pleasure and the frequency of their exchanges begins to increase.

After what we can assume have been several weeks the Head announces that a teacher will be visiting from Poland on exchange. That teacher is Steve. Carla is mortified, knowing that Steve will discover her real identity. Their correspondence ceases after Carla receives a letter from Steve, confirming his exchange visit. She thinks the tone is polite but cooler and she concludes that Steve feels rejected, having assumed her to be a teacher and aware of his imminent arrival, but having not volunteered to play host. She considers her options, including taking time off sick, but eventually persuades herself to stop worrying.

After Steve's arrival at the school and before Carla has met him she overhears a conversation between two teachers. Valerie Kenwood, who is playing host to Steve, speaks of him in a disparaging manner, criticizing his accent, his clothes (particularly his ties) and his preoccupation with literature. Carla then spots Steve in the canteen and summons up the courage to approach him, despite her feelings of guilt and inadequacy.

Steve, who is delighted to meet Carla contrary to her expectations, breaks into song. It is a song that Carla finally recognises from her early childhood. The story closes with the two of them singing in faltering duet much to the surprise of the Head.

Characters

Carla Carter

Although not mentioned in the story, we can assume from the omissions that Carla is a single parent, mother to only-child Jade. She describes herself in the first paragraph as "part-time catering staff, that's me £3.89 per hour." She is someone who is focused on her perceived standing in society and refers to herself continually in a self-deprecating fashion. Carla is a quiet woman but acutely conscious of her surroundings and her inner-monologue demonstrates a highly observant and empathetic nature. On occasions she can be sarcastic, scathing and quite child-like.

Stefan (Steve) Jeziorny

Steve is a polite young Polish teacher with a passion for literature and poetry. He is someone who enjoys sharing his passion as indicated by the contents of his letters to Carla. He is portrayed as a driven man with a humorous and optimistic outlook on life.

The scenes in the canteen reveal that he is not a judgemental person and that he too lacks confidence and self-esteem.

The Head

The Head is presented through Carla's narrative as a bumbling man, lacking in sincerity and with little knowledge of his staff outside the teaching fraternity.

Valerie Kenward

Valerie, Steve's host and a teacher at the school, is portrayed as a smug, greedy, highly critical woman, lacking in empathy. Her children appear to have inherited some of her worst traits. She is not someone to reason with and voices her opinions in a bullish way. Both she and the Head represent the anti-hero to the characters of Carla and Steve.

Language

The language used throughout the story is simple and colloquial. Sentences are short and contractions used throughout: "Somebody'd remember me...." This gives the story a very chatty and intimate feel. Steve's language, meanwhile, demonstrates that whilst his English is highly competent, it lacks the fluidity of native speakers: "You will know from your school, Carla, that I will come to England". Whilst it makes perfect grammatical sense, we would write: "that I will be coming to England".

Carla's use of language changes dramatically on meeting Steve. She begins to introduce similes: "He was tense as a guitar string" and "It went through me like a knife through butter". She also uses alliteration: "His big bright tie blazing".

The use of these poetic devices suggests an awakening in Carla, a determination to put aside her sense of inadequacy and to embrace her love of poetry.

Themes

Taken at its most literal and simplistic level, 'My Polish Teacher's Tie' describes how a school dinner lady rises above her personal inadequacies to explore her past and broaden her horizons. Steve provides the role of catalyst. A kind of alchemy ensues, arising from the collision of two worlds.

Sense of Self-worth

The theme of self-worth runs through the core of the story. Carla's self-worth or, rather, lack of it, is demonstrated by her acute awareness of her perceived social standing. In line 100 she identifies herself as being a separate entity from the teaching staff: "Colleagues don't wear blue overalls and white caps and work for £3.89 an hour". Similarly, on line 25 Carla recounts how "the meeting broke up and the Head vanished in a knot of teachers...." The use of the word "knot" in describing the collective of teachers again suggests that Carla perceives herself as an outsider and that the collective, the "knot", is impenetrable. In line 27 she observes that 'teachers are used to getting out of the way of catering staff without really seeing them'. She feels invisible.

Her opinions on the teaching staff are made clear by her omission in the opening paragraph: "I dish out tea and buns to the teachers twice a day, and I shovel chips on the kids' trays at dinner-time. It's not a bad job. I like the kids". She 'likes' the kids but makes no such comment on the teachers.

In line 22 she takes ownership of her lesser role: "I wrung out a cloth and wiped my surfaces", as if to say 'I know my place'. And in line 29, in trying to get the Head's attention she repeats "excuse me" three times, which serves to stress her invisibility. When the Head finally notices Carla, she recounts how he "stitched a smile on his face", suggesting that Carla finds him insincere and reluctant to engage with her. He then stumbles over her name and assumes that whatever she wants it means trouble: "Oh, er - Mrs, er – Carter. Is there a problem?" The hesitation in identifying Carla by name acts to highlight her sense of inferiority.

Similarly, in her relationship with Steve, she feels that without hanging on to the pretence of being a teacher he will become instantly disinterested, drawing her assumption from the attitude of the teaching staff around her. In line 106, having just been made aware of Steve's impending visit, she ruminates: "He'd think I was trying to make a fool of him, making him believe I was a teacher. Me, Carla Carter, part-time catering assistant, writing to him about poetry" (line 121-122).

Steve qualifies her interest in poetry; without him she feels unworthy to pursue her interest alone: "And then there was the poetry book I'd bought. It seemed a shame to bin it. It might come in use for Jade, I thought".

Loss and Retrieval of Identity

We learn that Carla is half-Polish very early on in the story. Her mother used to read rhymes to her, until her English father objected to her speaking Polish. She recounts her father's rationale in line 15: "You'll get her all mixed up, now she's going to school. What use is Polish ever going to be to her?" In line 13 she conveys how detached she feels from her Polish heritage: "I'm half-Polish. They don't know that here. My name's not Polish or anything...I spoke Polish till I was six, baby Polish...." Later in the paragraph she admits she recalls nothing of the language: "I can't speak it now. I've got a tape, a tape of me speaking Polish with Mum. I listen, and think I'm going to understand what we're saying, and then I don't".

Through her correspondence with Steve, she slowly retrieves some of her lost language and heritage but she also begins to identify herself as something beyond just a dinner lady. When they eventually meet in line 154 the layout of the dialogue breaks from convention: "'Hello', I said. He jumped up, held out his hand. 'How do you do?' he asked...'" Here both of them speak on the same line, which is entirely unique within the body of the story. Sharing the line evokes a sense of shared identity, a unification of two lonely souls.

The story closes with Steve breaking into song. It is a song that Carla recognises and she joins in. She is finally reunited with her past. With a renewed sense of self, she allows herself to be defined by who she is rather than what she does. The Head, astounded by the singing says: "Good heavens. How very remarkable. I didn't realise you were Polish, Mrs... er...". To which Carla replies: "Nor did I". The sentence continues with Carla's inner monologue: 'But I wasn't going to waste time on the Head. I wanted to talk about poetry. I smiled at Steve'.

The Imperialist Legacy

Valerie Kenward's scathing attitude towards Steve and her outspoken ridicule of his accent, clothing and conversation are all suggestive of a deeply entrenched sense of British superiority. Carla describes how "the Head was wagging a sheaf of papers in front of him (Steve), talking very loudly, as if he were deaf". This again indicates that Steve is perceived to be a lesser being. The theme is also touched upon in line 15 where Carla's English father dismisses the value of the Polish language and perhaps his daughter: "What use is Polish going to be to her?" The contempt shown towards Poland and Steve himself could be attributed to imperialism's legacy – an unspoken but continuing sense of national supremacy and prejudice.

Hope

Steve's garish tie symbolises a beacon of hope, both for himself and Carla, it could be seen to represent a breaking down of prejudice and social judgement. Both find themselves on the receiving end of discrimination. A particularly good example for Carla is when she requests the Polish teacher's address in line 33 and the Head fails to see her as a potential pen friend: "'I was just wondering, could I have that address?' 'Address?' 'The Polish one. You said there was a Polish teacher who wanted an English penfriend.' 'Oh. Ah, yes.' He paused, looking at me as if it might be a trick question.'"

Valerie Kenward provides the voice of discrimination in Steve's case

Carla acknowledges Steve's slightly unusual appearance: "He was wearing a brown suit with padded shoulders. It looked too big for him. His tie was wider than normal ties, and it was red with bold green squiggles on it. It was a terribly <u>hopeful</u> tie". Notice how Carla herself associates the tie with hope.

The final paragraph is symbolic of the breaking down of prejudice, Steve has accepted Carla for what she is, not what she does and the tie becomes a metaphor for a world without discrimination, a world with hope:

His red tie with its bold green squiggles was much too wide and much too bright. It was a flag from another country, a better country than the ones either of us lived in 'I like your tie,' I said.

A Note on Ownership

The title of the book suggests that the protagonist is a school child. The first line of the story is also indicative of this: "I wear a uniform, blue overall and white cap with the school logo". However, we quickly learn that Carla is a school dinner lady. The use of "My" in the title suggests a sense of ownership. Later in the story Steve will address Carla with: "'Carla! You are Carla Carter. <u>My</u> penfriend.'" This language of ownership acts to highlight the bond between the two individuals who, aside from their own mutual relationship, appear lost and unconnected to any social grouping.

A Note on Steve's First Poem

The first poem Steve sends to Carla describes a bird in a coal mine. It becomes trapped but continues singing until it eventually dies. Everyone can hear it singing, but no one can find it. Traditionally canaries were used as a warning system for toxic levels of carbon monoxide and methane. If the bird died it gave the miners sufficient time to exit the mine before they too were poisoned. In a sense Steve could be seen to represent the bird he describes. He has three things in common with the creature, he is in a foreign environment, he feels lost and yet despite this in the final paragraphs he breaks into song.

Steve, therefore, could be seen to represent Carla's canary, protecting her from her own poison – low self-esteem and a sense of not belonging.

'When the Wasps Drowned' – Clare Wigfall

Author

Clare Wigfall was born in Greenwich, London, in 1976, but grew up in California. She began writing at an early age and graduated from Manchester University in 1998. She then went and studied for an MA in Creative Writing at the University of East Anglia – a course which famous novelists such as Ian McEwan and Kazuo Ishiguro undertook. Faber and Faber offered her a publishing contract when she was 21. In 2007 her first collection of stories – *The Loudest Sound and Nothing* – was published and received many excellent reviews. She won the BBC National Short Story Award in 2008. She has travelled widely, and has lived in Morocco, Spain and Norwich. She now lives in Prague.

She has said of her stories: "When people ask what my stories are like I want to say they're like old folk songs. Spare and beautiful on the surface, but with a dark undercurrent if you listen closely to the lyrics."

'When the Wasps Drowned' comes from her first collection of stories. Very often the characters in her stories seem to be searching for something elusive and, as the ordinary events of the story unfold, a darker and more sinister side of life and human existence is revealed to the reader. This notion of things that have been lost or are missing is central to her stories. In 'When the Wasps Drowned' that which is missing – the body – is found, but the ending of the story is not happy because its discovery is linked to undiscovered crimes.

Plot

During the long summer break, while their mother works, Eveline has to look after her younger brother and sister: "Mum was out at work all day. She left us to our own devices" (line 35). One morning, as Eveline is washing up the breakfast dishes, she hears a scream coming from the garden. She looks out of the window to see her sister, Therese, rushing around the garden pursued by a swarm of wasps. Eveline disperses the wasps by turning the hose-pipe on them. Therese, it transpires, has trodden on a wasps' nest.

The summer is hot and their mother makes them wear flip-flops – prior to Therese being stung they had gone around barefoot. On some days they go to the park, but most of the time they laze around the family garden: Eveline sunbathes (a sign perhaps of her getting older), while Therese investigates the dead wasps, watched by Tyler.

In early August Therese and Tyler announce that they are going to dig to Australia and start to dig a hole under the wall adjacent to Mr Mordechai's house. Some time passes before Eveline notices a ring on her sister's hand. Curious to know where Therese has obtained the ring from, she discovers that Therese has dug it up from the hole in the ground that she and Tyler have been digging. They go the hole and when Eveline reaches in she touches something. Therese is sent for a torch and with it Eveline discovers a dead hand. The children fill the hole in and Eveline retains the ring, which she takes to wearing on her right index finger - but only when her mother is at work.

One day towards the end of the holidays, the quiet of the house is disturbed by the arrival of two police officers who call to ask questions about a missing girl. They show the children a photograph of the missing woman, but the children do not recognize her – but they also say nothing about the dead woman buried under the wall. Indeed, Eveline deliberately hides her right arm behind her back so that the police will not see the ring she has stolen from the dead girl's corpse. The children seem to find the police visit threatening: when Eveline opens the front door, "Therese and Tyler were both clinging to my bare legs' (lines 108 – 109). Eveline watches as the police officers make their way to Mr Mordechai's house. The children happily return to the garden.

Some readers feel that the ending of the story is inconclusive, but in one sense it is not. The police enquiries about the missing girl lead them to dig up Mr Mordechai's garden - something we have known about since line 20. There are unanswered questions, of course, which we deal with below in the section entitled "Dark Undercurrents" – one of the themes we have identified.

Despite the sinister nature of the dead girl buried in Mr Mordechai's garden and the terrible events that must have led to her death, the final sentence of the story is comforting in its tone: 'Taking Therese and Tyler by the hand, I turned , and we stepped back into the sunlight of the garden' (lines 128 -129). It seems to us that this sentence shows Eveline's desire to protect Tyler and Therese (she takes them by the hand) and leading them back to the 'sunlight of the garden' can be seen as positive image: she is taking them back into the innocence of the garden where they are safe from the dangers of the adult world.

Characters

Eveline

Eveline's age is not given, but she gives the impression of being in her early teens or even slightly younger, just on the edge of adolescence – she is certainly old enough to take charge of the other children. She is starting to show signs of growing older – making herself a bikini and being interested in boys, but she still goes to bed early while it is still daylight. She acts as a maternal figure to the other children. Despite taking on the role of the narrator, she reveals very little about her emotions either at the time of the events or now – as an adult looking back on them. This neutrality of emotions forces us as readers to take an active role in the story and decide for ourselves what the tone and mood and meaning of the story is.

Some readers see a sinister side to Eveline, but we disagree with that reading and interpretation. Of course, she should have reported the dead girl buried in the garden and she does steal the ring from the dead girl's hand – but her wearing of the ring is part of her 'playing' at being older – just as she makes herself a bikini, poses with sunglasses and uses the red dye from Smarties to imitate lip-stick. But Eveline is still a child and the discovery of the dead girl (who turns out from the photo the police show the children to be not much older than Eveline and wearing a bikini) makes her fearful of the adult world. On the first page of the story she tells us that was the first summer she had found the garden walls 'confining' (line 15) and at the park she sits by the swings and watches the boys. So, rather than seeing Eveline's behaviour as sinister, we see her as a vulnerable child, attracted to aspects of the adult world, but also deeply frightened by the dangers of the adult world in which young girls get murdered and buried in gardens. When they cover up the dead girl's arm, they are technically failing to report a crime, but we see Eveline as motivated by a desire to blank out the horror, not any sinister motive. After all, when Therese has nightmares about the arm growing up through the soil, Eveline shares and empathizes with her horror and shows her need for her mother: 'I wanted Mum's gentle shush in my own ear. When I closed my eyes I could see Therese's dream, the arm growing up through the soil' (lines 98 - 99). This is hardly the reaction of someone with sinister motives, we would suggest.

Therese

Therese is clearly younger than Eveline. She displays an ambivalent attitude to the wasps: frightened of them while they are alive and a potential threat and deeply fascinated by them when they are dead. Her action in starting to dig the tunnel shows she is more active and adventurous than the other children perhaps. She has terrible dreams about the dead body, but shows no emotion when it is first discovered.

Tyler

Tyler is the youngest and very dependent on Eveline for protection and guidance. He observes the others and generally does what they do. Wigfall does not make it clear whether or not he has seen the dead body, but Tyler clings to Eveline when the police arrive. He is under five, small enough to be pushed in a push chair.

Mum

The character of the mother is important, but important through her absence. We might assume she is a single mother and she is always tired; she wears a uniform but Wigfall does not reveal her occupation. Because of her absence, the children have the freedom to pursue their curiosity and the action of the story is able to take place. The children's father is never mentioned, but the mother clearly suffers from having to work full time – "She'd sit, her legs up on one of the kitchen chairs, complaining how her feet were swollen"(line 55). It is hard to be a single parent, but whatever has led to the father being absent – divorce, death, separation, abandonment – is never mentioned. Wigfall says of her stories that they contain a "dark undercurrent" and this one is resolutely ignored, but it is one of many dark undercurrents in the story.

Mr Mordechai

Mr Mordechai remains a mystery: he is never seen and only spoken about. Is there any significance to the fact that the body is found in his garden? Is he somehow implicated in the murder? We never know and Wigfall gives no hint.

The Setting

The story is set in an undefined past in late twentieth century England; Eveline is narrating the story as an adult looking back at the events of one summer. The details of transistor radios suggest a setting in the late 1960s or 1970s. The action of the story takes place in the family's house and garden, apart from one episode in the local park. Wigfall chooses not to describe the setting in any great detail: in a way, this house could be anywhere in suburban England. It may well be the summer of 1976 which suffered a very long and severe drought. Eveline comments early in the story about how hot and dry the weather is: "the sun shone every day and everybody commented upon it" (lines 2 – 3) and "the heat was all anyone ever seemed to speak of" (line 6), while Eveline admits she is "hungry for conversation" (line 4).

Language & Structure

The story is told in the first person by Eveline looking back on her childhood as an adult: this creates a special effect because her vocabulary and style are those of an adult although she is describing a childhood experience. She also knows what is going to happen, but chooses not to reveal all that she knows, immediately creating tension in the story. A good example of this is in line 20 where Eveline writes "That was the summer they dug up Mr Mordechai's garden". We have to read until the end of the story to discover exactly why Mr Mordechai's garden had to be dug up.

Symbolism

In the Christian tradition the Garden of Eden and Eve's acceptance of the apple from Satan, disguised as a serpent, brings death, decay and suffering into the world. In the Bible, Adam and Eve are expelled from the Garden, Paradise, and have to leave their innocence behind to enter the potentially evil and dangerous world of experience. This is clearly relevant to the story: at the beginning of the story, the children go barefoot but after the incident with the wasps their mother insists that they wear flip-flops.

It is not that the wasps symbolize anything specific: they are wasps, but they do represent the dangers of the real world. It is surely significant that the central character's name – Eveline is a modern variant of Eve. Like Eve who is tempted to eat the apple, Eveline looks over the garden wall, partly because she is tall enough, but also because she is curious about what is going on in the rest of the world – outside their garden: she comments in line 15 "It was the first time the walls had seemed confining". She is curious about the world that surrounds her now that she is "tall enough to peer" (lines 15 – 16) over the walls that surround the garden. When she is at the park with Therese and Tyler she tells us "…I'd sit by the swings and watch the boys. They'd stand in a huddle by the public loos, pulling on cigarettes" (lines 37 – 38). Although she does not state it explicitly, Eveline appears to be yearning for more contact with the adult world; she is passing beyond childhood and finds the "tinny music of distant transistor radios" (lines 17 – 18) beguiling – because they represent the adult world she is desperate to move into. Even her appropriation of the ring from Therese is part of this yearning to grow older: the description of the ring – "a thin gold ring, studded with small diamonds" (line 63) – suggests that it is an engagement ring and Eveline's wearing it on her finger seems to suggest a desire to be older than she is, to embrace the world of love and relationships represented by the ring and the boys in the park. She wears the ring to play at being a grown up, we might say.

At the same time, although she looks after Therese and Tyler, she does not really engage with them: while they obliterate the corpses of wasps, Eveline tells us "I'd watch them idly, lift an arm perhaps to point out another dead wasp lodged between blades of grass" (lines 44 – 46). Eveline sunbathes, wearing sunglasses she has bought herself and a bikini she has made from "a pair of pink knickers and an old vest which I'd cropped just below my nipples" (line 40) – which shows both her desire to grow up and her growing awareness of her own body. At night Therese and Tyler "were too hot and tired to feel they might be missing anything" and fall asleep early, but Eveline "would lie awake under the sheets, listening to the street and the muffle of mum's radio" (lines 91 – 93) – it is as though Eveline is anxious to find out everything about the world beyond the garden, the world she is so soon to join. At the same time she is wary: one night Therese has a bad dream and is comforted by their mother and Eveline shows that she is torn between childhood and adolescence by commenting "I wanted Mum's gentle shush in my own ear" (line 98). Eveline imagines the "arm growing up through the soil" (line 99) – the discovery of the corpse has shaken her.

Themes

Crimes Concealed

Whoever has buried the young girl beneath the wall is concealing a murder. Eveline does nothing about her knowledge and tells no-one: her only response is to help Therese and Tyler fill the hole in and then they forget about it. When the police arrive and show them the photo of a girl, she "held [her] right hand behind my back" (line 110 – 111), so that the police do not notice the ring she has taken from the girl. I don't get the sense that Wigfall intends us to blame Eveline for covering up the crime: in the final sentence of the story Eveline leads her younger brother and sister "back out into the sunlight of the garden" (line 129); it is almost as if Eveline has to lie to the police in order to satisfy a psychological need to deny that the world is the dangerous place it so obviously is. It is almost as if Eveline does not feel guilt about concealing the discovery of the corpse and, on balance, it is far better to stay in the garden where the only danger comes from wasps which can be easily killed with a hose pipe.

Spoken and Unspoken Danger

We all know the dangers of wasps: they sting and the sting hurts. What lies buried beneath the wall between the children's house and Mr Mordechai's garden represents the dangers of the adult world – which are also hinted at in the boys lolling and smoking in the park, and in the untold story of the children's parents' marriage. Perhaps even the ring and the commitment it shows to another person hints at the mysterious and bewildering complications of the adult world (to Eveline) in which girls and women are especially vulnerable. Perhaps the most important thing in the story which dies is Eveline's innocent curiosity about the adult world.

The Loss of Innocence and Death

Therese screams when she is stung by the wasps; the wasps die; the "late-teenage girl" (line 114) whose photo the police show to the children dies; the perfect garden protects the children from the dangers of the outside world – but only to an extent: the garden itself contains danger – the wasps – and the tunnel to Australia reveals the dead girl's arm. Even the sounds of life – the transistors – can be heard, intruding on the childish harmony of the garden.

"Dark Undercurrents"

Wigfall uses this phrase - "dark undercurrents" - to describe her own writing or the intended effect of her writing. In "When the Wasps Drowned" there are many dark undercurrents which arguably lead the end of the story to be disturbing and ambivalent. Where is the children's father? And what sadness and emotional trauma does his absence suggest? What experiences does Eveline have as she goes through adolescence and starts to get involved in relationships with boys like the ones she has seen in the park? What terrible chain of events has led to the murder of the teen-aged girl buried beneath the wall? Do the police catch the murderer? Who was the murderer? Who was the victim? In a sense, some of these questions are unimportant, because the real focus of the story is Eveline and her reaction – not just to the dead girl – but to her own burgeoning sexuality

What comes across most strongly from this story is the sense of the barefoot, innocent days of childhood being replaced, in Eveline's consciousness, by an awareness of the dangers and potential for hurt and pain of the adult world. Leaving the innocence of childhood is something with attendant dangers, summed up by the ring, which, although made of gold and covered in diamonds, still has "dirt lodged between the stones" (line 64) – a hint that all is not perfect in the adult world that Eveline is so keen to be part of, but which also scares her at the same time.

'Compass and Torch' – Elizabeth Baines

Author

Elizabeth Baines was born in Bridgend, South Wales and now lives in Manchester. She was once an English teacher but is now best known as the prize-winning author of plays for radio and stage and of three novels, *The Birth Machine*, *Body Cuts* and *Too Many Magpies*. Her short stories have been published widely in magazines and anthologies. *Balancing on the Edge of the World*, published by Salt in 2007 is her first collection of short stories, from which 'Compass and Torch' was extracted. It was pronounced a 'stunning collection' by *The Short Review*.

As well as being an author, Baines is also an active literary blogger (elizabethbaines.blogspot.com) and writes the well-known *Fiction Bitch* blog: fictionbitch.blogspot.com. She cites Nabokov, F Scott Fitzgerald and Margaret Atwood as her long-term inspirations. Of her work, Baines says, 'I'm interested in the unacknowledged, the edge of things.' She consciously explores and experiments with style and tone.

Plot

'Compass and Torch' is written in the third person and is set briefly in a house but predominantly in the moors and mountains. It is mainly written in the present tense and follows an intermittent pattern of prose – dialogue – prose. Very little happens in terms of action: the father collects the son, they walk up a hill and spend the night camping. The story is more concerned with sentiment and feelings. It is written from an omniscient narrative viewpoint which means that the narrator has access to all the characters' inner thoughts.

Briefly, 'Compass and Torch' concerns an eight year-old boy whose parents have separated a year earlier. For the first time in four months the father has access to the boy and he has planned a camping trip. The mother is disparaging of the father's plans and voices her concerns with her new partner, Jim. The boy overhears everything that is said as he readies himself for the trip.

With a mixture of excitement and trepidation the father and son set off.

When they arrive at the destination they begin gearing up. Their conversation revolves around three objects: a torch, a compass and a tent. The boy is anxious to please his father, whom he clearly dotes on. He worries about the fact that he has brought a torch but his dad has one too. Will this duplication make one of the torches redundant? Having established that two torches are better than one, the conversation moves to the tent. The boy is excited to learn that it is an 'all weather tent' but also a 'two man tent'. His father then reveals that he has forgotten to bring a compass; this reignites the boy's angst. He has a compass at home but did not bring it. We are then party to a large passage on the boy's inner worries. He also recounts how his mother's words, spoken in the kitchen with Jim, distracted him from his packing.

Throughout their time on the moors a pony is present, snooping into the boot of the car and nuzzling the rucksack top. Both father and son barely acknowledge the creature's presence.

Having organised all their camping items, the two set off towards the highest peak. When they reach their destination they set up camp. Having eaten their 'reconstituted' supper, the story closes with the boy chattering away until he falls asleep. The father's own angst about his child is then revealed. He fears that through the separation he has already lost his son.

While the two sleep, horses circle the tent. The author then tells us that for "years to come...in his dreams the boy will see their wild fringed eyes and feel the deep thudding of their hooves."

The story is essentially written from the boy's perspective, with brief insights into the father's thoughts and feelings. We are left to draw our own conclusions - did something sinister happen in the night? did the father and son become estranged following their trip? The author leaves these questions in our hands.

Characters

The boy

The boy is an eight-year old child who lives with his mother and her
new partner, Jim. He is acutely sensitive to all the adults around him
and it becomes clear that his parents' separation has had a profound
impact upon him. Nevertheless, he idolises his father; this is
apparent throughout the story. Line 135 provides an example: "Is it
the kind of compass where the top lifts up, like mine?' asks the boy
eagerly, with eyes only for the man." Line 8 also provides an
example of the boy's love of his father: "The boy is intent. Watching
Dad. Watching what Dad is. Drinking it in: the essence of Dadness."
He is also a very empathetic little boy, demonstrated by the passage
in which Jim admires his torch: "'It's a good one,' said Jim,
pointedly approving, handing it back. 'Yes,' said the boy, forcing
himself to acknowledge Jim's kindness and affirmation. But Jim is
not his dad."

The father

We know little of who the estranged father is or what he does in his
normal day to day life. Similarly we are never given the details
leading to the separation. What we do know is that he is a man trying
desperately hard to maintain a relationship with his son, to nurture a
rapport and to bond through their shared expedition. However, he is
not a man to discuss feelings; he allows the conversation to revolve
around the three objects. Despite this we know that he is a man with
very deep feelings for his son. In line 47 the author writes: "He is
looking away, seared by the glitter of anxiety in his little boy's
eyes." Towards the story's conclusion, in line 166 we are shown the
extent of the father's love and the anxiety attached to that love: "In
the plummeting darkness, the man's own anxiety began to mount.
He could feel it gathering in the blackening chill: the aching
certainty that already, only one year on from the separation, he had
lost his son, his child."

Jim

Jim physically plays a very minor role in this story. He represents
the altered dynamics of contemporary childhood, the step-father or
'Mum's new boyfriend'. We know little of him save that he remains
a quiet and vocally neutral party in the tense relationship between

father and mother and he demonstrates warmth and kindness to the boy.

The mother

The mother cares deeply for her son but her words suggest an acrimonious separation. When she appears in the story she is consistently belittling of the father. In line 101 the boy recalls his mother's words: "No hope of him relating to his son on any personal level! No hope of him trying to RELATE to him, full stop!" She speaks in the same vein in line 24: "'Well, what do you expect?' There was a choke in her voice now and suddenly a kind of snarl: 'You wouldn't expect him to start now, would you – accommodating his child into his life?'." She considers the expedition to be a "macho avoidance activity" which places the father within a very narrow and negative stereotype of masculinity.

The horse

The horse serves as a device to highlight the father and son's preoccupation with both their worries and one another. They fail to really see her and when she gets too close the father dismissively bats her away. On line 131: "The horse sighs. She wheels around. Facing the open moor, she lifts her tail, spreads her hind legs and provides a close up display which could easily fascinate an eight-year old boy: opens and flexes her bright-red arse and lets out a steaming stream." In the next line (135) the boy's lack of interest in anything beyond his father is clearly shown: "'Is it the kind of compass where the top lifts up, like mine?' asks the boy eagerly, with eyes only for the man."

Language

The language used throughout the story is simple; sentences are generally short and use of adjectives minimal.

In setting the scene, the author describes the surroundings using words associated with decay or damage. The 'bleached end-of-summer grass' which is 'bruised here and there'. Similarly the 'ancient rocks glint like heaving carcasses asleep'. The ponies are 'ghost coloured' and the lake is described as a 'black mirror'. The language used is suggestive of an underlying sadness.

Impersonal distant narration adds to a sense of estrangement; the boy is never named and the father is referred to throughout as 'the man'. Generally, the boy and man appear in separate and alternate paragraphs, which serves to support this sense of growing alienation. See-sawing of emotions together with shifts of narrative perspective also highlight the precariousness of the father and son's relationship. The prose literally swings from one character to the other almost like a hand held torch in the night or a compass needle. Line 84 through to 95 provides a good example, paragraphs open chronologically as follows:

The boy still chatters...

The man says with robust authority...

The boy is thrilled...

The man looks up...

The boy's eyes are suddenly wide...

But then the man says...

The boy breathes with relief...

The boy's emotional switches follow the same fluctuating pattern (line 88): The boy is thrilled... and line 91: "The boy's eyes are suddenly wide with fear and dismay" and then at line 95: "The boy breathes with relief..." These oscillating emotions create a sense of tension, and they stress how important the trip is to the boy.

Themes

Contemporary Childhood

The story involves the emotions associated with contemporary childhood, specifically the angst of the child. The boy wants to please all the adults in his life but feels torn between the separated parents. On line 117 the author describes the boy's split allegiance: "that brief but really awful moment when the car slid out of the drive and he felt, after all, he didn't want to go..." Lines 103 to 119 demonstrate how preoccupied he is with everyone else's happiness. He is highly attuned to the adults' interaction and observes the nuances of tone and mannerism. On line 104 the boy recounts: "...the way his dad said, 'Hi there!' in that brittle, jovial way to Jim, and the way Jim dropped his eyes when he'd said 'Hi' back..."And on his mother, he notes: "...the way his mother said hardly anything, and made her face blank whenever Dad spoke to her or looked her way, and kept shredding a tissue so bits leaked through her fingers to the floor..."

As a child of separated parents he is also deeply aware that while the trip is, or should be, a source of happiness for him; it provides the reverse for his mother: "her eyes were bulging and wobbly with tears, and he thought he couldn't bear this: that she didn't want him to go, that this moment which he had looked forward to, longed for, as his moment of joy, was a moment of unhappiness for her."

Throughout their trip the boy constantly seeks approval from his father. He tries to establish similarities between them, seeking reassurance of their relationship as father and son. Line 135 provides a good example: "Is it the kind of compass where the top lifts up, like mine?' asks the boy eagerly, with eyes only for the man". We can assume that these insecurities are a product of the parents' separation and the boy's limited contact with his father.

Fear of Loss

The mother, father and child all demonstrate a fear of loss. We know from the mother's emotions prior to the child leaving with his father that she fears loss and she verbalises these fears with Jim. She feels that the trip poses a physical threat to her young son. Meanwhile the boy's overwhelming desire to please his father communicates his fear of loss. And towards the end of the story we learn of the father's fears: "He could feel it in the blackening chill: the aching certainty that already, only one year on from the separation, he has lost his son, his child..." The boy and his father fail to communicate this mutual fear and it remains internalised right through to the end of the story. The final line of the story reads: "For years to come, though, in his dreams the boy will see their wild fringed eyes and feel the deep thudding of their hooves." If this is the boy's last memory of his time with his father, one assumption that we can draw is that the father's fear has transformed itself into a self-fulfilling prophecy of loss.

'On Seeing the 100% Perfect Girl One Beautiful April Morning' – Haruki Murakami

Author

Haruki Murakami was born in 1949 in Kyoto, Japan, the son of two teachers of Japanese literature. However, as a child he was exposed to Western culture and grew up listening to American music and reading avant-garde American writers such as Kurt Vonnegut and Richard Brautigan. After leaving university in 1973 Murakami and his wife ran a jazz bar in Tokyo for seven years and it was during this period that he wrote his first novel – *Hear the Wind Sing* (1979). He won a prize for this novel and has been writing and publishing ever since. Murakami and his wife left Japan in 1986 to travel in Europe until 1991 when they moved to the USA where Murakami lectured at Princeton University. They returned to Japan in 1995.

This story first appeared in the collection *The Elephant Vanishes*.

Plot

One morning the unnamed narrator of the story happens to see a girl approaching him whom he decides is the 100% perfect girl for him. He wants to talk to her but cannot think of anything to say which will not sound ludicrous or banal and so he says nothing and she passes by. They pass each other outside a flower shop and walk on. He turns after a few more strides, but she has disappeared. He tells someone at work what has happened to him, but the tone is casual and off-hand. The conversation implies that the narrator is alone, has no girlfriend and has had many infatuations with women in the past: his friend asks, "Your favourite type, then?" (line 20).

The narrator then goes back in time to tell a story which he decides is what he should have said to the girl. The story is about two teenagers who met fourteen years ago and believed that they were 100% perfect for each other. Murakami tells the story with great reverence for the wonderful thing that has happened to them: "It's a miracle, a cosmic miracle" (line 78). He paints an idyllic picture of their relationship:

They sat on a park bench, held hands, and told each other their stories hour after hour. They were not lonely anymore. They had been found by their 100% perfect other. What a wonderful thing it is to find and be found by your 100% perfect other (lines 75 – 78).

They agree on a test: convinced that they are perfect for each other, they agree to part, certain in the knowledge that, because they are each other's perfect partner, they will inevitably meet again. However, both the boy and the girl catch influenza and have their memories erased. They grow up into "truly upstanding citizens" (line 100) and they become "bright, determined young people" (line 97) whose "unremitting efforts" (line 98) allow them to become "fully-fledged members of society" (line 99).

But the effect of growing up means that at the end of the fourth section where they pass each other in the Harajuku neighbourhood of Tokyo (and replay the opening of the story again) they do so without any recognition. As Murakami comments "the glow of their memories was far too weak" line 113).

Characters

The narrator

We know hardly anything about the narrator – nothing about his family, his past, his name, his job, his friends, but short stories are economical and Murakami tells us all we need to know: he is thirty-two and is conscious that he is getting older; he is lonely and so desperate for female companionship that he fantasizes about approaching young women in the street and engaging them in conversation. He finds himself in restaurants "staring at the girl at the table next to mine because I like the shape of her nose" (lines 12 – 13). His lack of identity might be part of Murakami's message: that the young man's plight is an inevitable part of modern urban life.

The girl

We know even less about the girl in the story than we do about the narrator. He guesses she is thirty, but he can remember no specific details of her appearance, and feels that, like him, she is lonely and looking for love – but this is merely his fantasy of her. Rather light-heartedly he says he cannot remember whether she had a nose or not (line 15) which might suggest that his loneliness is such that he desperately wants her to be the 100% perfect girl for him, but he is so lonely that any female contact will do. Her appearance – even lacking a nose! – is not important.

The Setting

The story is set in April 1981. Spring is traditionally a time associated with new life and re-birth, growth and renewal – and a time of year associated particularly with people falling in love. The story is set in the Harajuku district – a very fashionable area full of stylish, modern and fashionable bars, shops and restaurants. It is exactly the type of area where two young people might hope to meet, but the bustling and lively streets are a marked contrast to the narrator's morose solitude.

It is worth remembering that Tokyo is a city of eight million people and it is at the centre of a larger conurbation which consists of over thirty-five million people: this puts the narrator's encounter with the girl and his hope to meet her again in sharp focus. The chances of his meeting the 100% perfect girl again are almost impossible.

Language and Structure

Murakami plays around with tenses in the course of telling the story:

Lines 1 -16 – he addresses the reader in the present tense.

Lines 17 – 26 – he switches to the past tense as he relates, apparently to a close male friend, the story of what happened with the girl – although, of course, nothing really happened.

Lines 27 – 58 – he describes the encounter with the girl, in more detail this time and also using the present tense.

Lines 59 – 115 - he tells the story that he wishes had happened, complete with what he really said to the girl. This is recounted in the past tense.

Lines 116 – 117 – he addresses the reader affectionately and ruefully, but with a sense of closure since he has, in the fourth section, satisfactorily concluded the story – although, of course, the ending does not change: even in this version the two young people ignore each other and pass each other without speaking.

In all but the fourth section, the language and tone that Murakami uses is light and colloquial. He uses several contractions – "she's", "I'd", "it's"; minor sentences – "Wish I could talk to her" (line 28), "Ridiculous" (line 40); the language he uses outside the fourth section is conventional, unoriginal and banal – his "mouth is as dry as a desert" (7 – 8); the spring morning is "really nice" (line 27). The reader is addressed directly as "you" which encourages us to empathize with him.

However, the fourth section stands out because it is in the past tense and is about the distant past as Murakami imagines what he should have said to her. The story he would have told her begins like a traditional fairy tale;

Once upon a time, there lived a boy and a girl. The boy was eighteen and the girl sixteen (Lines 64 – 65).

The characters in the fantasy story have no names, because they do not need them: in this fantasy fairy story they are generic characters and could be any young couple. What they say is highly stylized with frequent repetition – especially of the phrase "100% perfect". Unlike the real story that this story is embedded in, we are not told exactly where they are - which adds to the fantasy-like and slightly unreal nature of the encounter.

The flower shop may be important: it prompts the crazy possibility that he might buy her flowers on impulse and give them to her, but that spontaneous act would be seen as unusual and too forward. It is not something that we do to complete strangers and the narrator – for all his fantasy, is not crazy or impulsive.

The girl is carrying a letter which may be meant to indicate that she has someone to write to at least; the male narrator seems to have no-one. If she does have someone to write to, it may be a boyfriend or lover – a fact which the narrator, in his rather self-centred fantasy, has not taken into consideration at all.

Themes

Loneliness

The narrator describes himself as lonely; indeed, the very fact that he can spend so long thinking about a chance encounter in the street with an unknown girl shows how lonely he is. He describes the girl as lonely too: but that may be part of his fantasy, his delusion. He has to believe she is lonely in order for her to fit into his fantasy about her. For all he knows she might be in a happy and fulfilling relationship. Perhaps Murakami is inviting us to laugh slightly at the male delusion of the lonely female who will be instantly won over by his impressive story and his impassioned words. Certainly the narrator can imagine no response on the girl's part except for happy acquiescence.

Love, Fantasy & Reality

The notion that there is another human being out there who is just right for you is now rather quaint and old-fashioned. Many people have several relationships or even marriages in their lives. We are all human too, so the very idea of the 100% perfect girl can be seen as a type of male fantasy especially as the narrator decides she is the 100% perfect girl for him without having any communication at all with her and without being able to recall a single detail of her appearance. He is obviously very lonely and craves female companionship. Murakami intends this phrase "the 100% perfect girl" to sound slightly unrealistic and therefore amusing in its naivety. It shows how the narrator in his lonely, loveless state, retains a fantasy element about women and love. The brief exchange the narrator has with his friend or work colleague underlines this element of unrealistic and funny idealism: when the narrator announces "Yesterday on the street I passed the 100% perfect girl" (line 17), his friend/colleague's response is off-hand, "Yeah?....Good-looking?" (line18), which might even suggest this is a frequent occurrence.

Parallel Worlds

Murakami plays with the idea that the young man and the young woman might have had a parallel life, a different existence, happy and together, if only events and circumstances had turned out differently. This raises the tantalizing possibility for the reader of all the ways our lives might have worked differently if we had met different people at different times in our lives. This helps to create a sad and wistful tone to the story as it makes us think of lost opportunities and all the different ways our lives might have turned out.

City Life

It was said above that the setting is important. Cities are unusual groupings of people – unusual in that they contain millions of people who have no connection with one another at all. It is often observed that it is far easier to feel lonely in the city because you are surrounded by people – none of whom you know and with whom it is impossible to make a connection, beyond your small circle of work colleagues or friends. Furthermore, if you commute to work, as the narrator clearly does, in the course of a lifetime he will pass multitudes of people who are simply strangers and he will never exchange a single word with them. We might see the story as critical of this alienation from our fellow human beings that city life induces.

A Lament for Lost Innocence

We can detect in Murakami's words a wistful nostalgia for the past: in the fantasy section in the past, when the couple meet as teenagers, we are told that what has happened to them is a "miracle", but Murakami paints the effects of time in a negative, destructive light. The passage of time destroys the innocence that the young lovers once felt (in the narrator's imagined story of their alternative past). It is not simply the influenza which causes them to lose their memories; Murakami makes it clear that the process of growing older and conforming to society's expectations of how we should behave also plays its part: what Murakami describes as acquiring the "knowledge and feeling that qualified them to return as fully-fledged members of society" also, he suggests, involves losing the innocence and faith of youth. There are an even more telling couple of sentences which follow immediately:

Heaven be praised! They became truly upstanding citizens who knew how to transfer from one subway line to another, who were fully capable of sending a special-delivery letter at the post office. Indeed, they even experienced love again, sometimes as much as 75% or even 85% love (lines 99 – 104).

The mocking tone comes out in the first three lines – "Heaven be praised!" – and the complete triviality of the 'skills' they have achieved as adults (changing from one subway line to the next!) is hardly a great achievement. What is most important, and therefore most tragic, is that they have lost the ability to love 100%. This is what can happen as we grow older: we fit into the empty rituals of society, but lose our capacity to commit 100% and to believe in miracles.

The Ending of the Story

The narrator ends the story on what might be seen as a triumphant note: "Yes, that's it. That is what I should have said to her" (line 117). But is there really any chance of him saying that to her (or to the next perfect girl he sees on the way to work)? Probably not. In that sense the story ends on a slightly melancholy note, despite the narrator's optimistic tone – a note of innocence lost and happiness that will never be attained.

'The Darkness Out There' – Penelope Lively

Author

Penelope Lively was born in Cairo, Egypt in 1933 and spent the first twelve years of her life there. Her family then moved to England at the end of World War Two. In England she boarded at a school in Sussex before attending St Anne's College, Oxford where she read Modern History.

Lively, a prolific writer with over 40 published novels, has been the recipient of a host of literary awards during her writing career. These include the Carnegie Medal for the children's book 'The Ghost of Thomas Kempe' (1973), the Whitbread Children's Book Award for 'A Stitch in Time' (1976), the Arts Council National Book Award for 'Treasures of Time' (1979) and the Booker Prize for Fiction for 'Moon Tiger' (1987).

Her short stories have appeared in The Literary Review, Good Housekeeping, Vogue, Cosmopolitan, The Observer and the New York Times. She was awarded the OBE in 1989, the CBE in 2002 and the DBE in 2012. In 1998 she was awarded an honorary doctorate from the University of Warwick.

Describing the purpose behind her writing she states: 'In writing fiction I am trying to impose order upon chaos, to give structure and meaning to what is apparently random. People have always sought explanations and palliatives for the arbitrary judgements of fate. I am an agnostic, and while I would not suggest the construction of fiction as an alternative to religious belief, it does seem to me that many writers – and I am certainly one – look at it as an opportunity to perceive and explain pattern and meaning in human existence.'

Lively's work is especially concerned with history and memory. She perceives memory, not in the context of a chronological time frame, but as an assortment of mental slides. 'The Darkness Out There' is a short story extracted from the collection *Pack of Cards,* published in 1984.

Plot

'The Darkness Out There' is written in the third person. It is set in the English countryside and in the home of an elderly widow. It begins with paragraphs of narrative, however, as the story progresses the narrative gives way to dialogue.

In the story school-girl Sandra (the protagonist) is a member of the Good Neighbours' Club. A club set up to help the elderly amongst the community. Miss Hammond, or Pat, who runs the Good Neighbour's Club assigns Sandra to help Mrs Rutter for the afternoon. As Sandra makes her way along a path to the elderly lady's cottage the narrative turns to Packer's End; a dense spinney at the edge of the path. Steeped in local folklore the woods hold a long-standing intrigue and association with menace. We learn that when Sandra was small the woods were thought to contain witches, wolves and tigers, later in childhood she became aware that a German aircraft had crashed in Packer's End. As a child you never went into Packer's End alone.

As Sandra progresses towards Mrs Rutter's home she bumps into Kerry Stevens, a boy from her school who has also been asked to help Mrs Rutter. When they have finished the various tasks Mrs Rutter has asked them to attend to they sit down to drink some tea. Mrs Rutter then recounts the story of the German aircraft.

The aircraft crashed into Packer's End on what Mrs Rutter describes as a 'filthy wet night, pouring cats and dogs'. She and her sister were alone in the house when it happened. They went to investigate and found that one of the crew was still alive but 'hurt pretty bad'. Mrs Rutter then tells the children how they left the airman unattended in the crashed plane for two nights. She gives a number of reasons for failing to notify the authorities: 'it was bucketing down, cats and dogs,' she discovered that her bike had a flat tyre and Dot her sister was 'running a bit of a temp'. She had, in fact, no intention of helping the airman for whom she displays utter contempt and mercilessness. In line 325 she tells the children:

I reckon he may have seen me, not that he was in a state to take much in. He called out something. I thought, oh no, you had this coming to you, mate, there's a war on. You won't know that expression – it was what everybody said in those days. I thought, why should I do anything for you? Nobody did anything for my Bill, did they? I was a widow at thirty-nine. I've been on my own ever since.

The children, appalled at her story and her treatment of the young airman, leave the house almost immediately. The story closes with Sandra's realisation that things are not always as they initially seem.

Setting and Time

The story is set in the countryside and in the home of Mrs Rutter, regional dialect is used but it does not establish exactly what part of the country the story refers to. Similarly, we know that the story was written in 1984, however, some of the references within the story suggest that time is a little more ambiguous. Sandra refers to Kerry as a 'stupid so-and-so' in line 82 and in line 251 when the German plane is brought into the conversation she confesses 'it always gives me the willies.' She dreams of a life rather more redolent of the 1950s, citing amongst her ambitions secretarial work. Both her language and expectations feel dated for 1984. Perhaps this is testimony to the author's age and the limited possibilities which would have been available to her as a young girl.

Characters

Sandra

Sandra is a girl with quite unremarkable and vague expectations of life. She tells Kerry in line 207 that she wants to be a secretary and in line 67 she relays her dreams: "She would fall in love and she would get a good job and she would have one of those new Singers that do zig-zag stitch and make an embroidered coat." We can assume that Sandra is at secondary school and on the cusp of puberty, the paragraph beginning at line 125 suggests a sexual awakening: "The girl blushed. She looked at the floor, at her own feet, neat and slim and brown. She touched, secretly, the soft skin of her thigh; she felt her breasts poke up and out at the thin stuff of her top..." We know that Kerry is due to start work in July of the same year so, as his peer, we can deduce that Sandra is about fourteen or fifteen years' old.

She is quite a stereotyped version of a girl with her aversion to dirt and her perceptions of neatly classified male and female roles. Line 201: "She thought of the oily workshop floors, of the fetid underside of cars. She couldn't stand the feel of dirt, if her hands were the least bit grubby she would go and wash. And at line 208: Men didn't mind so much. At home, her dad did things like unblocking the sink and cleaning the stove..." Similarly, she happily accepts the tasks Mrs Rutter assigns to her, which are quite different to the typically male chores assigned to Kerry. Sandra identifies herself as a nervous character, line 176: "She was nervy, she knew. Mum always said so."

In the story Sandra's innocence gives way to a greater worldliness. She is used as a tool to demonstrate that things and people are not always as they seem. She demonstrates a shift from imagined child-hood fears to real horror at the atrocities of adulthood: "You could get people wrong and there was a darkness that was not the darkness of tree shadows and murky undergrowth and you could not draw the curtains and keep it out because it was in your head, once known, in your head for ever like lines from a song..."

Kerry Stevens

We learn through Sandra that 'none of her lot reckoned much on (him)'. She describes him as having black-slicked down hair and slitty eyes. Volunteering her opinion of him she concludes that "Some people you only have to look at to know they're not up to much". However, Kerry is a young man who has volunteered his services to the elderly, so at once there is a tension between Sandra's analysis and the readers' own. On his physical appearance the narrator discloses that "his chin was explosive with acne; at his middle his jeans yawned from his T-shirt showing pale chilly flesh."

Kerry undertakes his assigned tasks without complaint and reveals to the old woman his equally modest ambitions to start working at the Blue Star garage with day release at 'the tech' after he has left school.

On learning of the airman's plight Kerry is the first to demonstrate outrage. While Sandra is clearly upset, Kerry's anger is palpable and manifests itself both verbally and physically: "The boy said, 'I'm not going near that old bitch again.' He leaned against the gate clenching his fists on an iron rung; he shook slightly. 'I won't ever forget him, that poor sod.'"

Pat/Miss Hammond

Pat plays a very minor role in this story, she is used as a device to set the initial scene. In the opening paragraph she describes Mrs Rutter in a way that suggests that she is both sweet and fragile: "Mrs Rutter at Nether Cottage, you don't know her, Sandra? She's a dear old thing, all on her own, of course, we try to keep an eye on her. A wonky leg after her op and the home help's off with a bad back (line 4)." As the story progresses this character analysis is challenged and finally reversed.

On Pat's physical demeanour, in the second paragraph we can assume that Sandra has adopted the role of narrator, she describes Pat: "Pat had a funny eye, a squint, so that her glance swerved away from you as she talked. And a big chest jutting under washed-out jerseys (line 9)." Sandra muses: "Are people who help other people always not very nice-looking?"

So whilst Pat is clearly not a physically attractive person, she is a very caring person. However, in paragraph five Pat's caring nature is shown to be tempered with a lack of social sensitivity: "The old folks, Pat called them. Pat had done the notice in the library: Come and have fun giving a helping hand to the old folks. Adopt a granny. And the jokey cartoon drawing of a dear old bod with specs on the end of her nose and a shawl. One or two of the old people had been a bit sharp about that (line 20-23)."

Mrs Rutter

Mrs Rutter's age is not directly stated but by deduction we can assume that she is in her mid-eighties. The story was written in 1984, if we assume that 1984 is the present day and she was 39 at the start of the war (line 329) when her husband was shot dead (line 165), Mrs Rutter would be approximately 84.

As mentioned above, Mrs Rutter is initially portrayed as a dear old lady, fragile and in need of help. Her house is filled with sentimental china ornaments: 'big-eyed flop-eared rabbits and beribboned kittens and flowery milkmaids and a pair of naked chubby children wearing daisy chains' (line 102). All these visual clues suggest a sweet and gentle-natured lady. However, as the story progresses layers are pealed back to reveal a more sinister nature. When Kerry discloses his plans to start at the garage after finishing school, Mrs Rutter responds with: "Well, I expect that's good steady money if you'd nothing special in mind. Sugar?" Here she demonstrates a demeaning and dismissive side. Later, talking of Pat, she passes further judgement: "She was down here last week. Ever such a nice person. Kind. It's sad she never married."

When she finally recounts the story of the crashed German plane, she displays a long-standing bitterness, an uncompromising sense of blamelessness and an utter lack of regret. She even recalls that she, along with others, took 'souvenirs' from the site of the crash, as if the incident was little more than a day trip. While the airman is left dying in the plane Mrs Rutter recounts how she attended to her chores before going back into the woods to 'have another look'.

We learn that the airman is not an old man as Mrs Rutter initially imagined but a young man, around the age of twenty and yet Mrs Rutter, oblivious to the irony of her words, states twice in the story that she has an empathy with young people. Once at line 170 before she has recounted the story of the German plane: "*I* like young people, I never had any children, it's been a loss that, I've got sympathy with young people." And at line 342, after having shared the German soldier's plight: "I like having someone young about the place, once in a while. I've got sympathy with young people."

That Mrs Rutter fails to recognise the irony of her words suggests that the young airman was, in her eyes, an almost sub-human adversary, not a living breathing person. When the children decide to leave she is almost stunned, unaware of their shock and revulsion: "'Eh?' said the old woman. 'You're off are you?'... (line 340)."

Language

The narrative passages within the body of the story switch style. Sometimes we are party to the author's words and at other times the narrative is written from Sandra's perspective. The author achieves this by alternating between two distinct methods. The first, which supplies the author's perspective, uses formal language, complex metaphors and pronouns in place of the characters' names. This creates a sense of detachment and adult authority. The second method, which supplies Sandra's perspective, uses truncated sentences and a simpler more casual use of words, suggestive of her age. The extracts below provide a good example:

The author as narrator:

Line 95: "She seemed composed of circles, a cottage-loaf of a woman, with a face below which chins collapsed one into another, a creamy smiling pool of a face in which her eyes snapped and darted."

Line 138: "When she returned, the old woman was back in the armchair, a composite chintzy mass from which cushions oozed and her voice flowed softly on."

Sandra as narrator:

Line 40: "It was alright out here in the sunshine. Fine."

Line 186: "A place in the country. One day she would have a place in the country, but not like this. Sometime."

The author uses metaphor liberally throughout the story, this serves to paint a very detailed visual picture. In line 96 the author describes Mrs Rutter's face as: "...a creamy smiling pool of a face..." and in line 116 describing the surroundings she writes: "Beyond, the spinney reached up to the fence a no-man's-land of willowherb and thistle." Simile is used to the same effect – line 128: "a speck like a pin-head"; line 109: "Her eyes investigate, quick as mice."

Colloquial language is used throughout the story, both Sandra and Kerry speak in regional dialect (line 82): "'Kerry Stevens you stupid-so-and-so, what d'you want to go and do that for, you give me the fright of my life'. He grinned. 'I seen you coming. Thought I might as well wait.'" Similarly, Mrs Rutter alternately addresses Sandra as "my duck" or "dear".

The author uses repetition to emphasize the atmosphere. Towards the beginning of the story several permutations of 'sun' are repeated: Sunshine; sunburn; hair was hot from the sun; glinted in the sun. These are all words or phrases associated with lightness, they are not suggestive of the darkness which will manifest itself later in the story. By way of contrast in the penultimate paragraph the author repeats the word 'darkness'. This repetition serves to emphasize the horrors of what the two children have learnt: "You could get people wrong and there was a darkness that was not the darkness of tree shadows and murky undergrowth... One moment you were walking in long grass with the sun on your hair and birds singing and the next you glimpsed darkness, an inescapable darkness. The darkness was out there and it was part of you..."

Darkness and light are used as metaphors for good and bad. At first the darkness is attached to Packer's End but later in the story we understand that the darkness refers to an 'inescapable darkness', that is, the darkness of human nature.

Themes

The Deception of Appearances

Perhaps the main theme running core to the story is that appearances are deceptive, things are not always as they may initially seem. The author first presents the scene as pretty, flower filled and sun-drenched, an innocuous atmosphere: "pollen summer grass that glinted in the sun." However, she then introduces Packer's End, a complete contrast. The woods are menacing and full of folklore and horrors, both imagined and real: "It was a rank place, all whippy saplings and brambles and a gully with a dumped mattress and bedstead... And, somewhere, presumably, the crumbling rusty scraps of metal and cloth and... bones?"

The characters also follow this theme. At first we are lead to believe that Mrs Rutter is a 'dear old thing', however, later in the story she reveals her true colours when having found the dying airman she recounts her actions: "He was hurt pretty bad. He was kind of talking to himself... Dot said he's not going to last long, and a good job too, three of them that'll be. She'd been a VAD so she knew a bit about casualties, see.' Mrs Rutter licked her lips; she looked across at them, her eyes darting. 'Then we went back to the cottage.'" Far from being a 'dear old thing', Mrs Rutter shows herself to be unapologetically ruthless.

Similarly Kerry is initially presented as someone Sandra and her friends have no time for, Sandra certainly makes clear her disappointment when she realises that Kerry will be helping out with her at Mrs Rutter's: "She wished there was Suzie to have a giggle with, not just Kerry Stevens." He is described unsympathetically as having "black licked-down hair" and "slitty eyes", his chin is "explosive with acne". However, when he learns of the airman's plight his demeanour changes. He becomes physically and verbally demonstrative. His language becomes peppered with swear words. Appalled at the airman's treatment he says: "I'm not going near that old bitch again".

Sandra finally recognises Kerry as the young man he is, no longer is he someone to be 'not reckoned much on' and no longer does she perceive him as immature (line 216: "She considered him, across the fence, over a chasm. Mum said boys matured later, in many ways"). In the penultimate paragraph the author divulges Sandra's new attitude:

She couldn't think of anything to say. He had grown; he had got older and larger. His anger eclipsed his acne, the patches of grease on his jeans, his lardy midriff. You could get people all wrong, she realised with alarm.

The final paragraph summarises this core theme: "She walked behind him, through a world grown unreliable, in which flowers sparkle and birds sing but everything is not as it seems."

The Darkness and the Light

This is an important theme, so much so that it is part of the story's title. There is a physical contrast between darkness and light: the journey in the sunshine and the darkness of Packer's End. But there is also the metaphorical contrast between darkness and light, the contrast between good and evil.

Looking Forward/Looking Back

In the story Sandra dreams of the future. Her imagined future is a simple one: to fall in love, to have a couple of children, to work as a secretary and to have a little cottage in the country. As she prepares for her visit to Mrs Rutter she muses innocently: "Now, she would go to this old Mrs Rutter's and have a bit of a giggle with Susie and come home for tea and wash her hair. She would walk like this through the silken grass with the wind seething the corn and the secret invisible life of birds beside her in the hedge..." Here she paints an idyllic and undemanding picture of the immediate future, her thoughts are full of hopes and desires. This is in direct contrast to Mrs Rutter's retrospective thinking. Mrs Rutter speaks only of the past and she delivers her thoughts with bitterness and regret. Perhaps her thoughts remain in the past because after her husband's death, her life appears to have gone into stasis. She does not re-marry, she has no children and she continues residing in the marital home.

A Note on Stereotyping and Prejudice

Sandra reveals herself to hold a number of subliminal prejudices. Namely: People who help other people are not very nice looking, while people with platinum highlights and spike-heel suede boots are unlikely to offer community support. Similarly, when she reflects on events at Packer's End she recounts that the attackers of a young girl were 'two enormous blokes, sort of gypsy types.' Sandra slots herself into a very narrow stereotype with her dreams of secretarial work, becoming a home-maker and a mother. Her aversion to dirt and her concept of male work suggest an acceptance of really quite old-fashioned and gender divisive thinking.

Meanwhile Pat bundles all old people into a 'dear old thing' category, referring to them as 'the old folks' and encouraging support for the Good Neighbour's Club with the advert 'Adopt a granny'. Effectively, she defines people purely by their age.

Mrs Rutter's prejudice is transparent. She refers to the injured airman as 'that Jerry'; her self-professed empathy for young people evidently does not extend to the German.

'Anil' – Ridjal Noor

Author

Ridjal Noor was born in 1979 and lives in Singapore where he runs a design firm. He cites R K Narayan and V S Naipaul as the influences on his writing. He has had several short stories published.

Plot

In a poor and remote village in rural Malaysia, the young boy called Anil is awake in the middle of the night. He's gazing through a hole in the roof of the family's hut at a star. He is aware of his mother asleep and then snoring next to him. Soon, through the writer's description of his life, we get a sense of how poor the family is: there are many holes in the roof; his father is a bully who physically abuses his mother; we are told that Anil would have the time and the sensitivity to gaze at the star he sees through the hole in the roof.

Anil's father is a servant to the headman, and it is established in the opening of the story that when he grows up Anil will also be expected to serve the headman: in this sense the course of Anil's life is already mapped out for him, although he is unaware of this.

As he lies there he becomes aware of a desperate need to urinate, but he's frightened to go outside into the dark. As a young boy he finds the darkness frightening in general, but also believes that there are ghosts outside the hut which may capture him and also that there is a large tree in the village which captures young children with its long branches and reels them in before eating them. He is torn between his desperate need to go to the toilet and his fear of the darkness.

He becomes aware of a voice outside calling Marimuthu - the name of the village headman's brother. Anil goes to the window to see what is going on. At first he can see the scary tree that he believes captures and eats young children, but slowly his eyes become accustomed to the darkness and he is aware that he is watching two men (Marimuthu and someone else) hoist the covered body of a woman into the tree. As he watches more, Anil realizes that she has been unconscious, but the pain of the noose around her neck and the imminence of death bring her back to consciousness before she very quickly dies. Anil goes back to crouch in the corner of his parents' hut his body wracked with sobs, while "the rest of the village slept and dreamt little dreams".

When he wakes in the morning the family hut is deserted, and there is a "noisy commotion outside the hut" (103 - 104). The noose is hanging from the tree, but the body has gone, and his parents are part of a large circle of villagers gathered around the tree. Anil pushes his way through the circle of people to find the dead woman on the ground; the headman's mother is there, crying over the corpse, and so is the husband of the dead woman – Marimuthu - whom Anil has seen murder her. The headman authoritatively announces that it is clear that his sister-in-law has committed suicide by hanging herself and that because of this there is no need to involve the authorities. The other villagers seem to agree, although there is some speculation about what might have caused Marimuthu's wife to commit suicide. Anil is at the front of the crowd and whispers to Marimuthu, "You killed her. You killed your wife." (159 – 160). At this point in the story the headman of the village intervenes and takes Anil's father, Ragunathan, and drags Anil to his house to discuss the situation.

At this point there is a break in the story and we move to the afternoon of the same day. Ragunathan is seeing his son off on a train: he is being sent away to the big city to be privately educated and trained to be a professional. It is clear that the headman is happy to pay for Anil's education in order to get him out of the way because Anil witnessed the murder of Marimuthu's wife. Both Anil and his father are clearly upset at this sudden and abrupt departure. The train leaves the village as the woman's body is being burnt, and Marimuthu "heaved a sigh of relief" (226) and the headman has "the shadow of a smile about his lips" (225) as Anil's departure effectively means that they have got away with murder.

Characters

Anil

In many ways Anil is a typical seven-year-old boy: he is afraid of the dark; he believes the fanciful stories and rumours spread around the village concerning the tree and its powers to eat children; he is frightened of his father and doesn't want to wake him in order to go to the toilet; he attempts to wake his mother knowing he will get a more sympathetic response, but is unsuccessful; he has little idea of his future – he doesn't know at the start of the story that he is destined to become servant to the headman just as his father and mother are. But in other ways he is very different from the rest of the villagers. We are told early in the story that the villagers are asleep "dreaming their dreams that rarely amounted to anything" (3 - 4):

Probably a new cow for Kuppusamy, the milkman, or a profitable harvest for the farmers, or a new sewing machine for Rajgopal, the tailor (4 – 5).

These are mundane, everyday dreams – despite their importance in the poverty of the developing world. By contrast, Anil is different. His gazing at the star through the hole in the roof of his parents' hut is given significance by Noor who comments:

He found the star fascinating. His parents would not even stop for a second to gape at a star. But he did. Because he believed in the magical wonders of life. Because his dreams were bigger than him. (lines17 – 20).

The events of the story prove Anil slightly naïve about the magical wonders of life, but his departure at the end of the story can be seen to represent one dream – the dream of escape from this poverty-stricken and corrupt village, although it is bitter-sweet from a personal point of view as it wrenches Anil away from his parents and all that he is familiar with; on a moral level too, his departure to a prestigious school in a distant city comes at the cost of covering up the crime of murder.

Ragunathan

Ragunathan, Anil's father and servant to the village headman has no dreams like Anil's and is completely subservient to the wishes of his master. He physically abuses his wife – Anil notices (29) the bruise on her shoulder from where his father had hit her the previous night when he returned home drunk; Anil does not dare waken his father to accompany him outside to urinate which also suggests, perhaps, a distance in their relationship: Anil reflects, "He did not need a walloping at this time of the night" (40) which suggests that he frequently hits Anil. More insidiously, Ragunathan is always ready to support the headman without question. Noor describes him as "a burly man, a bully to his family and a timid mouse to the headman" (38 -39). When the headman decides what has happened and that the authorities do not need to be called, we are told, "Anil's father was one of the first to agree" (144). As the headman asks Ragunathan to accompany him with Anil to the headman's hut after Anil has revealed that he knows the truth, we are told, "And Ragunathan, the illiterate, uneducated father, the person with little dreams, a mouse of the man who was ever ready to serve his employer, nodded agreeably" (179 – 180). However, Noor allows Ragunathan to redeem himself when he says farewell to his son on the train. At this point Noor reveals that Ragunathan has been ashamed "to hide the truth about Marimuthu's wife's death" (199), but that, despite having been such a bully to Anil, he has acted in his son's own interests, but still feels a sense of guilt for doing so:

Was it wrong that he had sacrificed the truth and justice for his son's only chance out of an otherwise dreary life like his? (lines 201 – 202)

This is an interesting development by the writer because it shows a moral sensitivity that we would not have guessed Ragunathan possessed and it encapsulates the moral dilemma he has faced.

The headman

The headman plays an important part in the plot: he controls it, just as he controls what happens in the village, but he is not portrayed with any detail. He is simply an authority figure who is used to getting his own way through power, influence and intimidation. In a sense he is allowed to do this because no one in the village is prepared to stand up to him. Noor is surely commenting on the way village politics are corrupt and allow those in power to cover up crimes like murder and do exactly as they wish. We never find out why Murimuthu has murdered his wife: what is important in the story is that he is allowed to get away with it.

The Setting

The setting of the story is rural Malaysia, an impoverished part of a developing country. The lives of the villagers depend on the land and they have very limited ambitions; all authority is wielded by the headman. He makes references to the "authorities" (142), presumably the police, but they have no influence whatsoever on the course of justice in the village, so a murder is covered up as suicide and two murderers get away with their crime. The village is very poor: the huts let in the rain, the villagers' clothes are old and shabby. In this sense, the life of education that awaits Anil is a welcome escape, but the ending of the story has a bitter-sweet tone as we shall see and is filled with irony.

Structure and Language

Noor tells the story as a third person omniscient narrator, but the narrative viewpoint is always that of Anil until the final two paragraphs of the story where we see things from the point of view of the headman and his brother. This change of focus seems to suggest that nothing will change in the village in the future and that Anil and his knowledge of the truth of the murder are safely out of the way. The story is divided into two sections: a long section which describes the events of the night and the following day when the body is discovered; and a much shorter one which describes Anil's departure and the burning of the dead woman's body. The crucial meeting in the headman's hut between the headman, Anil and Anil's father is left undescribed, but we can work out exactly what was said at that meeting from the ending of the story: Anil has been offered the opportunity to have an education in a city school provided he keeps quiet about the truth of what he has seen.

The opening of the story sounds almost like the opening of a fairy story - "On a hot, sweltering night… there was a little village" (1 - 2), although the mosquitoes' "reign of terrorism" could be said to introduce a slightly sinister note.

The story ends in irony, because Anil is the only one who knows the truth about the murder, but also because he is benefitting from it. The irony is double-edged too because something very good is happening to Anil – he is escaping the poverty and bullying of the village (exemplified by both his father and the headman), but this wonderful thing is happening because another human being has died and, what is even worse, the politics of the village have ensured that her murderers will escape any punishment.

There is also something very moving about his departure: his father may be a bully, but being sent to the city for many years and being torn away from everything he knows is still a very disturbing experience and Anil is clearly upset: "Anil looked up at his father and nodded, tears swimming on the rims of his eyes. His lower lip trembled" (186 -187). Ironically his father chides him: "Men don't cry. You're going into a man's world, you must act like a man now." This is ironic because Ragunathan has been described as a mouse throughout: he does not stand up to the headman as a real man would. His father shows real emotion as the train picks up speed and Anil saw "his father fall to his knees, a bent, despaired figure that had just let go of his only son" (214 – 215). Anil's last thought as he watches his village recede in the distance is "I will never forget this town and the sin that it buries today" (216 – 217). Perhaps in this we may see some hope for the future: if he becomes a lawyer (one of the professions his father has urged him to think of) then perhaps one day in the future he can bring the headman and Marimuthu to justice.

Themes

Dreams and Imagination

The opening paragraph draws attention to the mundane dreams of the villagers and Noor develops this idea when he describes, as a contrast to the villagers, Anil's heightened sensitivity in looking at the star. The star itself might be seen as a symbol of ambition, given Anil's destiny at the end of the story: we talk about reaching for the stars to describe ambition and aspiration. However, Anil's childish imagination is also able to summon up images of horror. He believes, as do all the children of the village, that the tree regularly eats children. This imagined horror becomes ironic since the tree is used to hang Marimuthu's wife and therefore becomes a source of real horror, not imagined childish fantasy.

Women and the Power of Patriarchal Society

Women in this story are the victims of men and have no power whatsoever. Indeed, they are the passive objects of male violence. Marimuthu (with the help of another man – is it the headman himself?) murders his wife; Ragunathan regularly beats his wife. Both the main male adult characters are presented as bullies. The headman arrogantly believes he can act as he wishes and, in a sense, the story shows that he can. Anil and his father can be bought off and their silence ensured because of the headman's power and wealth.

Brutality and Violence

The murder, its cover up and the domestic abuse that Anil and his mother suffer are typical of a patriarchal and corrupt society which uses violence to get its own way. The mosquitoes' "reign of terrorism" in the opening sentence which introduced a sinister note turns out to be justified in the light of events in the story. Indeed, given such a violent atmosphere, the reader might wonder at Anil's fate when he is first led off to the headman's hut: what might happen to him in this violent village where the headman's power is unquestioned.

Poverty

The story draws attention to the appalling poverty in remote parts of developing countries and implies as well that the village's apparent remoteness and poverty means that the headman is able to exercise justice as he likes because of his power over the other villagers, power that is based on his position and his wealth.

'Something Old, Something New' – Leila Aboulela

Author

Leila Aboulela was born in 1964 in Cairo but grew up in the Sudan in the city of Khartoum. She has some claim to fame as the daughter of the very first female demographer in Sudan and Aboulela herself graduated with a degree in Economics from Khartoum University in 1985. After graduation she moved to London and studied at the London School of Economics to complete a Masters degree in Statistics. When she married she moved to Aberdeen because her husband worked on an offshore oil rig. It was in Aberdeen that she began to write – finding consolation in writing about the Sudan, which she sees as her homeland. At the moment she lives and works as a lecturer in Abu Dhabi.

Aboulela has written two novels which have both been highly praised by critics, and she has also written many short stories. Although her writing is not strictly autobiographical, it often focuses on the Sudan and she seems to like to explore the mind-sets, emotions and the psychology of people who follow Islam. Broadly speaking we might say that her fiction concentrates on a conception of being human and being alive that mostly transcends race, nationality, gender and class. Given her background – studying in London, living in Scotland, now living in Abu Dhabi – there is often a sense of cultural and geographical displacement in her work. We might say that the clash of cultures in 'Something Old, Something New' is a motif characteristic of her writing which she frequently returns to.

Plot

The story begins when a young Scottish man arrives at Khartoum Airport in the Sudan. It is clear that is it is his first journey abroad and he is nervous: not simply because he is in a foreign country, but also because he is about to meet his fiancée's family for the first time. Everything seems strange to him. He's met at the airport by his Sudanese fiancée accompanied by her brother of whom he is rather wary and who seems to treat the young Scotsman with a mixture of amusement and contempt. The man is taken by car to the Khartoum Hilton Hotel where he's going to stay until the couple's marriage. They discuss her need for a visa in order for her to leave the country with him as his wife.

In a flashback it is revealed that the couple met in Edinburgh when she was working as a waitress, after prayers at her mosque on Friday evening. The Scotsman had dropped out of university and then converted to Islam. She was in Edinburgh because she had gone to Scotland to marry her first husband, but they are now divorced due to her husband's infidelity.

As the story progresses the Scotsman meets his wife's family and is taken on various excursions, on which they are always joined by family members. He feels a little restricted by the constant presence of her family and is clearly frustrated at not being able to spend time alone with her. In a violent street mugging his passport and his camera are stolen and he reacts very angrily, but she is embarrassed by his reaction. However, she too becomes angry after a visit to the British Embassy where she is confronted with an unsympathetic bureaucratic response.

On their return to the family house they discover that her uncle has died and, according to Islamic tradition, three days of mourning follow. The couple are not allowed to meet at all during this period of mourning, which adds greatly to the man's frustration and puts the plans for their wedding in some doubt.

The man and the brother have a long conversation after the period of mourning and, after the Scotsman has given the brother more money, it is finally agreed that the ceremony will be held, without a party or any big celebration (out of respect to the dead uncle), very quietly and privately at the brother's flat.

Everyone is assembled and dressed for the wedding, the Imam is present and filling in the marriage certificate and then, in a hilarious episode just as the ceremony is about to take place and the couple's dreams are about to be fulfilled, the Imam refuses to marry them because the Scotsman does not have an Islamic name. After prolonged discussion and debate, the Imam is finally convinced when the Scotsman recites the Fatiha, the opening chapter of the Koran.

Finally, at the end of story, once the period of mourning is over, the couple get married in a simple Islamic ceremony performed in her brother's flat, and at last they are alone and together in their own room at the Hilton Hotel. The ending is completely happy and forward-looking.

Arabic Words

Salamu alleikum – Peace be upon you

Insha'Allah – God willing

Azan – the call to prayer

Makkah – also known as Mecca, a holy city in Saudi Arabia – a site of pilgrimage for Muslims

Mosque – Islamic building of worship

Allah – the Arabic word for God

Ka'ba – the holiest site in Islam – a cube-shaped building inside the grand mosque in Makkah

Jellabiya – a traditional Arabic garment

Sheikh – a respectful term meaning 'elder' and used by Muslims to describe Islamic scholars

Fatiha – the opening chapter of the Qur'an or Koran, the holy book of Islam

Imam – an Islamic priest

All these Arabic words help to convey a sense of a culture alien to British readers. However, at the same time, Aboulela makes the occasional reference to Western culture: describing the aged uncle as "Bill Cosby's look-a-like" (lines 223 & 240) and *The Godfather II.* This works in two ways: it shows how we increasingly share some aspects of culture across the world, but it also gives her Western readers a reference point.

Characters

The man is clearly clever: at school we are told he was always top of his class and he went on to study at university. However, he dropped out of medical school and at that point his life lacked direction until he converted to Islam. His new faith has given him renewed purpose in life and the desire to marry and start a family. In many ways his trip to the Sudan is very brave – he finds the whole experience rather alien and unsettling; for example, he becomes angry when things go wrong and frustrated because he and his fiancée never get the chance to be together. We know that despite his conversion to Islam and the courage that must have taken, that he is actually quite timid: early in the story in the flashback that describes how the couple met, Aboulela warns us that "He was cautious by nature, wanting new things but held back by a vague mistrust. It was enough for the time being that he had stepped into the Nile Café, he had no intention of experimenting with weird tastes" (lines 86 – 88). In the final lines of the story he admits that the experience has been a rough one.

The woman originally went to Scotland in order to get married to a Sudanese man who was living in Edinburgh. There is a clear suggestion that the marriage was an arranged one and this is not unusual in Islamic cultures. However, her husband was unfaithful (he already had a live-in English girlfriend), and he and the woman were very quickly divorced. As readers our perceptions of the woman are filtered through the feelings and perceptions of the man at all times: he sees her as beautiful, dignified and calm, but his own sense of low self-esteem allows him to believe that at times she is laughing at him. She herself shows an emotional side when she gets frustrated and angry because of her visits to the British Embassy. At the end of the story, when asked by her new husband if she feels sorry for him, she admits that she does. This shows her awareness that his Scottish culture and her Sudanese culture can be difficult to reconcile with each other, but also suggests that the marriage will be successful.

The woman's own family are very close to each other and very protective of her. Since her first marriage ended in divorce, they are likely to be suspicious of her new husband – especially since he is a foreigner and a convert to Islam.

The woman's brother seems rather threatening to the man because he always seems to be interested in money – this arouses the man's suspicions about whether he, as the relatively wealthy Westerner, is being exploited. However, the brother can be seen as being genuinely protective of his sister and is regretful that the family arranged the woman's first marriage to a man who was unworthy of her: her brother calls her first husband "that son of a dog", showing his contempt for him (line 439 -440). Everyone knew that the first husband had a British girlfriend but they hoped that by arranging for him to marry a Sudanese woman, he would give her up and commit himself to married life. Because he didn't the brother's protectiveness towards his sister is understandable perhaps. By the time of the wedding the Scotsman and the brother seem to get along all right. Significantly, after all the men have prayed together at the mosque after the period of mourning for the woman's dead uncle, we are told, "In the car there was a new ease between them, a kind of bonding because they had prayed together" (lines 371 – 2).

The uncle who later dies is amusing and benevolent: he is compared to Bill Cosby, a black American comedian – a simile which is used by Aboulela to suggest his sense of humour, but also to give her Western readers a point of reference; he is also very proud of an English song he knows about cricket. However, his death is used by Aboulela to make clear the family's traditional Islamic values and to stress the difference between Scottish and Sudanese culture. The funeral and the period of mourning also put further strain on the couple's relationship, because they have no communication whatsoever and do not see each other for several days.

Language & Structure

The title of the story alludes to the traditional rhyme that prescribes that brides on their wedding day should wear "Something old, something new, something borrowed, something blue", but clearly can be interpreted in different ways in the light of the story. What is 'old' in the story? Love between a man and a woman; a family's desire to protect their daughter; the culture of Sudan; the traditions of Islam; the tensions between different cultures. And what is 'new' in the story? The love between the man and the woman is new and is going to result in marriage. In a sense marriages across race and culture, while not completely new, are still a fairly modern phenomenon. For the man much is new: he is overwhelmed with new impressions of a country he has never visited before, some of them good, some less favourable. Is anything borrowed? The man has 'borrowed' Islam in the sense that it is not native to Scotland, but his new-found religious faith is shown in a positive light. Blue? The man's first sight of the Nile – a river that is iconic and famous in world culture – is picked out by Aboulela as important and significant: "And there was the Nile, a blue he had never seen before, a child's blue, a dream's blue" (lines 45 – 46). But his mixed feelings about the Sudan are also present in his feelings about the Nile: he recognizes its beauty, but also that its "flow was forceful, not innocent, not playful. Crocodiles no doubt lurked beneath its surface. He could picture an accident: blood, death, bones" (lines 48 – 50).

The story is told in chronological order, but there are flashbacks to events in Edinburgh which tell us more about the young man's past and about the beginnings of their relationship. These flashbacks are a vital part of the story because without them we would not know that the woman has been married or why she divorced or even why she was in Scotland working in a restaurant. As far as the young man is concerned, the flashbacks explain his crisis in life after he dropped out of medical school, his conversion to Islam and his meeting and courtship of the woman: if he had not converted to Islam, he would not be eating in the restaurant which is so close to the mosque. There are also moments when, faced with something typically Sudanese, such as the hard, dry earth that they dig the Uncle's grave in, the man thinks back to events in Scotland and the sheer difference between the two countries and their customs and climates.

The story is told in the third person with Aboulela as the omniscient narrator – 'omniscient' simply means all-knowing, so she knows everything about the characters and writes about them as if she is watching them. However, Aboulela often gives us the point of view of the Scotsman and very rarely that of another character, perhaps because he is observing so many things for the first time, so it is natural to give us his perspective. In addition, Aboulela is writing in English for an English-speaking audience who have probably not been to the Sudan and may therefore share some of the young man's doubts and fears, as well as his wonder at seeing the River Nile. Aboulela also makes extensive use of dialogue: we hear what characters say and form an impression of their characters from their words.

The man and the woman are never named. This seems to be a deliberate ploy on Aboulela's part to suggest that they could be anyone: that what is important about them is that they are a man and a woman who love each other and who want to be together, and, therefore, all the differences – different nationality and culture – and the obstacles that are put in their way – the delay to the marriage, the mugging, the attitude of the British Embassy staff – are unimportant compared to their love. The story of the love between a man and a woman is as old as the earth.

Aboulela uses many Arabic words in the story – chiefly to do with Islamic customs or food and drink – to keep the idea of a different, alien culture in the forefront of the reader's mind. Because the Scotsman has converted to Islam and also really enjoys all the food he tries this helps build a very positive picture of a different culture and, more broadly, encourages us to feel that the marriage will be a success once they can be alone together.

Themes

Being Abroad

The opening sentence of the story prepares us for the sense of alienation that the Scotsman feels at being abroad in a country which is so different from his own: "Her country disturbed him" (line 1). Throughout the story Aboulela frequently reminds us of how alien another country can be to a newly-arrived tourist. Early on the Scotsman thinks to himself, "I will get used to the dust… but not the heat. He could do with a breath of fresh air, that tang of rain he was accustomed to" (lines 25 - 26). His first car ride from the airport seems to confirm his prejudiced stereotypes about the lack of discipline in foreign traffic: "It was like a ride in a fun fair. The windows wide open; voices, car-horns, people crossing the road at random, touching the cars with their fingers as if the cars were benign cattle" (lines 32 – 34). He is especially fearful of being robbed:

Anyone of these passers-by could easily punch him through the window, yank off his watch, his sunglasses, snatch his wallet from the pocket of his shirt (lines 34 – 36).

His fears are realised later in the story when he is mugged on the street: his rucksack is slashed open and his passport and camera are stolen. Aboulela describes this incident as "the eruption of latent fears, the slap of a nightmare" (line 274). The Scotsman is very angry, but begins to calm down when they report the theft at the police station which "was surprisingly pleasant" (line 290) and where they "were treated well, given cold water, tea" (line 291).

This fear of being mugged abroad is not uncommon for single travellers – in any foreign country, and his anger at being robbed is mirrored by her irritation at the way the staff at the British Embassy treat her when they go to get a new passport and apply for the woman to have an exit visa as his wife. She says that the embassy staff were insinuating that she stole his passport and feels that the staff were sneering at her as if she were only marrying him in order to get out of Sudan and back to Scotland. On both sides there is mutual distrust based on stereotypes: abroad everyone is a potential mugger and foreign women marry UK citizens to get a visa for entry to the country.

However, there are other parts of the Scotsman's Sudanese experience which he relishes and enjoys: the Nile, the food and fruits, and being in an Islamic country – all of which he finds fascinating and interesting.

In the wake of the robbery and their visit to the British Embassy, the Scotsman is tempted to leave and return to Scotland, but Aboulela tells us "something else made him stay" (line 334 – 335) – and that something else is his profound love for the woman.

Concepts of Islam

Islam is presented in a largely positive light in the story. It is true that the woman has entered an arranged marriage which ended in divorce after six months, but she says that she wanted to love her new husband: it was his infidelity that stopped the marriage from working. When the man arrives at Khartoum Airport he is not allowed to kiss his bride-to-be and they are not allowed to be alone together until after their marriage, but this is presented more as part of Sudanese culture and tradition rather than an inherent part of Islam: his desire to kiss her at the airport suggests strongly that they have kissed before in Edinburgh, but there has been no other intimacy between them: the story later reveals that he has never seen her hair since the Islamic code of dress dictates that her hair should be covered at all times. Similarly, the period of mourning for the woman's uncle makes the man irritated by the further delay to their marriage – but this is a cultural custom rather than part of Islamic belief. When she first realizes that he has converted to Islam she is astonished: "Why on earth did you convert?" she asks him (line 165), because she associates Islam "with her dark skin, her African blood, her own weakness" (lines 166 – 167) and because she sees Muslims as "the wretched of the world" (Line 168). By contrast, he associates Islam with "elegance and reason" (line 409).

In other respects, Islam is presented as a force for good, because it has changed the young man's life and given him purpose. Having failed to make the grade as a doctor, we are told:

His get-up-and go had suddenly disappeared, as if amputated. 'What's it all for, what's the point?' he asked himself. He asked himself taboo questions. And really, that was the worst of it; these were the questions that brought all the walls down (lines 117 – 120).

But he finds his answers in Islam and begins to lead a productive life. He faces bewilderment and dismay from his parents because he converts to Islam, but Aboulela makes it clear that the alternatives are much worse. Given his failure at medical school and his questioning of the meaning of life, it would have been easy for him to be "sucked up into unemployment, drugs, depression; the underworld" (lines 174 – 175). His parents are aware of "their neighbour's son [who] hanged himself (drugs of course and days without showering). There was a secret plague that targeted young men" (lines 176 – 178). In this sense, Islam is presented as a good thing because it saves the man from the "secret plague", the path of self-destruction that other young Scotsmen choose.

Poverty & Wealth

Because Sudan is a developing country much of the population is desperately poor. We are reminded of this throughout the story. The woman is proud that they have booked him into the Hilton Hotel because although the country is poor, they do have a luxury hotel. The Scotsman is always wary that he is going to be cheated out of money – because he has so much compared with the poverty in the Sudan. He shows his naivety when he is approached by a street beggar:

A small boy touched his arm, begging. Gnarled fist, black skin turned grey from malnutrition, one eye clogged with thick mucous (line 315 – 316).

Faced with this raw evidence of the poverty of the developing world, the Scotsman tries to give him a 200 dinar note – which is excessive; his bride-to-be reproaches him for his innocence: "Are you out of your mind... giving him that amount? He'll get mugged for it" (lines 319 -320).

At another point the man reflects on his wife-to-be's childhood and youth growing up in Sudan and realizes:

... for the first time, the things she'd never had: a desk of her own, a room of her own, her own dressing table, her own mug, her own packet of biscuits. She had always lived as part of a group, part of her family (lines 232 – 324).

These details remind us of the poverty of the developing world, but also suggest that the materialism of Western culture is only superficial and not completely satisfying – after all, the man has had all these things, but has completely lost all purpose in his life before his conversion to Islam.

Subservience of Women

The woman's first marriage has been an arranged one and has only ended because of the woman's insistence and because her husband would not give up his British girlfriend for the sake of his marriage. During the period of mourning, the sexes are kept completely apart, the women mourning in private and out of sight, the men receiving the visitors in the tent in the garden. Islamic and Sudanese custom dictates that the man and the woman cannot even kiss or be alone together before they are married.

The Ending of the Story

What is the final impact of the story? If we look at the closing paragraphs, the story suggests that the marriage will be successful and that despite all the delays and difficulties the couple have been subjected to, because of the clash of cultures and their different nationalities, the marriage will be successful. They have successfully overcome the obstacles they have faced and are married with a life of love and togetherness ahead of them. When he sees her after the marriage he says, "God, I can't believe it!" so astonished is he by her beauty and "those dark slanting eyes smiling at him" (line 530); for the first time he sees her hair "long and falling on her shoulders" (line 531) and, despite all the things he wants to say to her "He was stilled, choked by a kind of brightness" (line 546). His final act – as well as becoming aware of "how soft she was... [and] how she smelt" – is to insist that she should not wear gloves in Edinburgh to conceal the henna tattoos on her hands: this small act is significant because it shows that he accepts her fully for who and what she is, and that the marriage will be successful.

In the end, despite all the difficulties they undergo, the moments of tension and irritation between them, and the Scotsman's fears of the foreignness of the Sudan and that he is being exploited, this is a love story. He finds much in Sudan that is alien and disturbing, but we should not forget the end of the opening paragraph:

...he was driven by feelings, that was why he was here, that was why he had crossed boundaries and seas, and now walked through a blaze of hot air from the aeroplane steps to the terminal (lines 4 – 6).

As a whole then this is a story about the triumph of love between two human beings, despite all the boundaries they have to cross. Aboulela's decision not to name the man and the woman can therefore be seen as an attempt to give their story a universal significance: they are a man and a woman deeply in love with each other – and that story is as old as humanity itself, despite the modern details of aeroplanes and Hilton hotels, air conditioning and difficulties with visas. By giving them no names, Aboulela is suggesting that they could be any man and any woman at any time and from any country who are strongly moved by love.

Model Answers

In English and English Literature it is impossible to write a 'model' answer, because there are countless ways to write a good answer that will achieve a high grade. As a subject, English thrives on different opinions and individual insights – your own personal response. However, through teaching we come across a lot of students who say, "I have no idea how to start" or who have deep responses to a particular story but are unsure about how to put their ideas down on paper. So what follows are answers to questions asked by the exam board on the anthology in 2011 and 2012 – not perfect answers at all, but examples of what might have been written. If we have used words you do not understand, it is to encourage you to use them. There are some golden rules to remember when you write on literature: quote often but keep your quotations short and always comment on them; answer the question and use the words that the examiner uses in the question; do not write about the characters as if they are real people – they are not – they are imaginary creations of the writer; try to show an awareness of other interpretations – if something in a story is unclear or capable of being interpreted in more than one way, have the confidence to say so – provided you are answering the question.

The questions at Foundation and Higher Tier do differ in each examination session, and they also differ in that Foundation Tier questions use slightly simpler language and bullet points. We, however, make no distinctions below between the two tiers as the structure of the questions is essentially the same, as are the assessment objectives. We have kept the answers that follow to around one thousand words: they are not 'perfect' answers (such things do not exist in English Literature) and we could have written much more, but we are conscious that you have only a very limited amount of time to answer the question in the examination.

On the exam paper you have a choice of two questions: you answer only one. Each question has two parts. Part (a) of each question will ask you to consider an aspect or a feature of a named story in the anthology, so you have no choice about which story to write about. Part (b) will ask you to consider the same aspect or feature, but relating it to a story of your choice from the anthology. In our model answers we do the choosing in part (b) for you, but in the brief notes that follow each model answer, we do point out alternatives that might have been used. It is important that you choose for part (b) a story that works – given the demands of the question. Just glance now at the first question below: part (a) asks about Baines' use of symbolism in 'Compass and Torch'; part (b) asks you to consider symbolism in another story: there is no right answer to this, but not every object in every story is symbolic, so you do have to think before you answer part (b) to make sure you are choosing a story that is appropriate and that will give you enough material to write about. On this exam paper there is no requirement for you to compare the two stories that you write about – you get no credit if you do so.

One final piece of advice: it is very important that you write roughly equal amounts on both stories, on both (a) and (b). In bold in the mark scheme that examiners use it states: "To achieve a mark in Band 3 or higher candidates should deal with both parts of the question. To achieve a mark in Band 6 candidates should offer a substantial treatment of both parts". Band 6 is the highest band. In the model answers that follow, we have tried to write roughly equal amounts on each part of each question. Make sure you leave yourself enough time to answer the second half of the question.

Question 1

Part (a) Write about the ways Baines uses the symbols of the compass and the torch to convey important ideas in 'Compass and Torch'

The mother's overheard words in line 19 indicate that the boy and his father have become estranged, following the parents' separation: "Mad! The first time in four months he has his eight-year-old son and what does he plan to do?" Baines introduces the torch, then the compass, as tools used by the boy to identify with his father. He is trying to establish similarities, to reinforce or recreate their bond as father and child. In line 61 Baines writes: "Have you brought one too, have you brought a torch?", then in line 75: "What colour is your torch?" and at line 95 the boy's attention is turned to the compass: "I've got a compass," he cries, "and guess what, I forgot mine too!" The attention the writer attributes to these inanimate objects creates a sense that they are pivotal to the bonding.

However, whilst the father and son are clearly anxious about their relationship the dialogue revolves almost entirely around the objects. In a sense they provide an alternative focus or a distraction from the real issues and fears both parties feel. But rather than raise these mutual feelings, both parties remain silent. We know that the father is aware of the boy's angst because on line 47 Baines writes: "He is looking away, seared by the glitter of anxiety in his little boy's eyes." However, rather than address this directly the father uses the torch as a means to reassure his child. Line 69 refers to the duplication of the torches: "The man is gratefully caught on a wave of triumph. 'Oh, yes, two are definitely better! Back-up for a start'". As a reader, knowing through the omniscient narrative of the shared anxieties, the characters' attention to the objects feels misguided and this in turn creates a sense of frustration because deeper, more salient emotions are left neglected.

The author has chosen two items whose purpose is to guide the way, to illuminate a route when it is unclear. These devices provide a metaphor for what the father and son so desperately need, guidance and the ability to directly address their fears. But rather than vocalise their concerns which could provide the key to cementing their relationship, ironically, their attention is focused not on one another directly but on the physical objects.

Towards the end of the story Baines uses the compass as a means of conveying the boy's innate hopefulness : "But they don't need a compass after all. They are adventurers, after all. Compasses are things that boys and dads tend to have, but which, when they are alert and strong at heart, they can leave behind. It is no accident that they both "left their compasses behind" (line 120). This is in stark contrast with the father's doubts, which the author demonstrates in line 165. Here the absence of light, the metaphorical torch, and the growing darkness reflect the father's sentiments: "...the man failed to light it first time and the flare sputtered and died. In the plummeting darkness, the man's own anxiety began to mount. He could feel it gathering in the blackening chill: the aching certainty...he has lost his son, his child". Finally, at line 171: "The man gently takes away the torch". This could be seen to symbolise the father's defeat; he is removing from his child the object that the boy has so desperately employed to establish mutual similarities.

Part (b) Go on to write about the ways in which symbolism is used in one other story in the Anthology

In 'When the Wasps Drowned' Clare Wigfall uses symbolism to chart how the long, hot summer starts to go wrong and also to show the narrator's slow growth to awareness and adulthood.

The opening sentence mentions Therese stepping on the wasps' nest and later her screaming causes the narrator to drop a glass in the kitchen: Wigfall writes, "it broke the day" (lines 24 – 25) and brought an end to our barefoot wanderings (lines 2 – 3) – which itself could be seen as symbolic of their innocence. Before the breaking of the glass and the detail of Therese's reaction to the wasps, the narrator, Eveline, has made it clear that these events took place in an exceptionally lovely and perfect summer: "The heat was all anyone ever seemed to speak of" (line 6) and "The chemist sold out of after-sun that summer, and the flower beds dried up, and people had to queue to get in the swimming pool" (lines 9 – 10). At the same time the narrator is clearly growing up: it was the first summer, she tells us, that the walls of the garden seemed "confining" (line 15). The first section ends with the sentence: "That was the summer they dug up Mr Mordechai's garden" (line 20) – but exactly why his garden was dug up is not revealed until later in the story.

Symbolically, it is as if the garden represents childhood and the perfect summer weather reflects the happiness and innocence of childhood, while the wasps and other details gradually introduce more threatening, more sinister elements into the narrator's life, so that by the end of the story, her innocence has been destroyed. However, the narrator, who is looking back at these events many years later, is very reticent – she offers very little emotional reaction to what happens and Wigfall allows us very little insight into her thoughts. On their own these things would not be symbolic, but taken together they give us a hint that unpleasant, evil things can happen in the adult world. The narrator, in addition to finding the garden walls "confining", is clearly growing up: she is acutely aware of her own body - she sunbathes in a skimpy home-made bikini, "cropped just below my nipples" (line 40); she has responsibility for her younger brother and sister; she notices the boys in the park "puffing on cigarettes" (line 38); she refuses to help Therese and Tyler when they decide to dig to Australia; when Therese finds a ring in the ground the narrator wears it – but takes it off before her mother returns. Eveline seems to want to grow up and leave childhood behind, but does not really face up to this – which is perhaps why she is so reticent about her feelings.

The defining moment is not only the discovery of the dead body in the tunnel leading into Mr Mordechai's garden; it is also Eveline's decision to fill the hole back in and not to tell anyone about what they have discovered: this symbolises her fear of the adult world that she is about to enter. The police finally call with a photo of a missing girl – presumably the girl whose body is buried in Mr Mordechai's garden. The children plead ignorance and Eveline holds the hand wearing the ring behind her. Then, in a symbolic attempt to shut out the dangers of the adult world, "we stepped back into the sunlight of the garden" (line 129).

'When the Wasps Drowned' is about the difficult transition to adulthood, and it uses many symbolic elements. The perfect summer and the garden itself are symbolic of childhood, but the wasps, the boys in the park, the children's mother's own single status and, most dramatically, the corpse in Mr Mordechai's garden are symbols of the potential pain and misery in the adult world.

Note

We have used 'When the Wasps Drowned' for part (b), but 'Anil' would have been a good choice because the child-eating tree that Anil fears so much could be said to symbolise the corrupt way his home village is run and the genuinely evil events that occur in the story. In addition, Noor uses the star that Anil gazes at through the hole in the roof of the family hut to suggest that Anil is more thoughtful than the other villagers and is somehow destined for great things in life – which in a sense comes true because at the end of the story he is on his way to the big city and an education at a prestigious school. In Murakami's 'On Seeing the 100% Perfect Girl One Beautiful April Morning' the girl that the narrator fantasizes about could be seen as a symbol of lost innocence or perhaps a continued faith (on the narrator's part) in the possibility of a pure and uncorrupted relationship. She certainly seems to symbolize the purity and innocence that are lost in the passage to adulthood.

Question 2

Part (a) Write about the ways Baines presents the relationship between the boy and his father in 'Compass and Torch'

From the beginning of the story the boy's adoration of his father is clear. Baines writes in the opening paragraph : "He is watching the man: the way he strides to the gate...his calf-muscles flexing beneath the wide knee-length shorts...." (line 4). She continues: "The boy is intent. Watching Dad...drinking it in: the essence of Dadness". The boy is described in terms that suggest he is attuned and aware of every detail of his father; his oscillating emotions also suggest that he is acutely attentive to what his father may be feeling throughout the story and his happiness depends entirely upon his father's own mood. On line 10 "the boy misses a breath" but by line 15 "the boy is relieved". Similarly by line 64 "he is uncertain, potentially dismayed", but then at line 68 he gives a "swoop of delight". The writer unambiguously describes a child who is anxious to please.

Both the man and the boy are presented as being oblivious to their surroundings, despite the fact that they are in the country and surrounded by horses and wildlife. When on line 131 the horse "lifts her tail, spreads her hind legs and provides a close-up display which could easily fascinate an eight-year-old boy; opens and flexes her bright-red arse and lets out a steaming stream", the boy is preoccupied not with the horse's display but with his father's compass (line 135). Similarly at line 57 "neither man nor boy takes much notice of the horse", and again on line 78 "Unseen by man and boy, clouds sweep like opening curtains...." While the boy's focus is almost exclusively on his father, the father appears lost in his own thoughts and anxieties.

As they arrive at their destination Baines describes how the man is "looking away, seared by the glitter of anxiety in his little boy's eyes" (line 47), and when the boy struggles to open his rucksack the author describes the man's response "his chest twist(s)" (line 128). It is not until the closing paragraphs that Baines explicitly reveals the depth of the father's angst and the strength of his feelings for his son. At line 164 she writes: "In the plummeting darkness, the man's own anxiety began to mount. He could feel it gathering in the blackening chill: the aching certainty that already, only one year on from the separation, he has lost his son, his child..." Whilst father and son share this mutual anxiety, the author concentrates the dialogue not around personal fears but around the compass and the torch. The compass and torch could be seen to symbolise objects that are capable of guiding the way when a journey or route is unclear. However, rather than providing guidance, they operate to detract from the issues at the forefront of both their minds: that of loss and losing the way. This irony serves to amplify the sadness of the relationship between boy and father and the potentially damaging omission from their conversations of their reciprocal fears of losing one another.

And then part (b) Write about the presentation of a relationship from one other story from Sunlight on the Grass

The relationship between the man and the woman in 'Something Old, Something New' is presented in an interesting way by Aboulela. In one sense the couple are very constrained because they are Muslim and because the story takes place in the Sudan: they are not allowed to be alone together, despite the fact that they are soon to be married, and Aboulela frequently reminds us of all the difficulties they face. On the other hand, in a very restrained way, we are reminded that they clearly have deep feelings for one another, even though their religion and the customs of the country they are in do not allow them to show these deep feelings.

When the man first arrives he says, "I mustn't kiss you" (line 9) and she confirms this: "No... you mustn't" (line 10). In the car drive from the airport he does not sit with her and they cannot have an intimate conversation "not least because her brother understood English" (line 30 – 31). This inability to demonstrate their emotions causes tensions between them, especially from the man's perspective. On the car drive Aboulela writes, "... suddenly it seemed to him, in a peevish sort of way, unfair that they should be separated like that" (lines 27 – 28).

Generally Aboulela, although writing as an omniscient narrator, gives us the man's perceptions and feelings. As the story continues the man often becomes frustrated at never being alone with his wife-to-be, and the death of her uncle and the subsequent period of mourning makes the situation worse – they do not even see each other for several days and have no communication. On the day that he is mugged and she is patronised by the staff at the British Embassy he is so upset that he thought of giving up and leaving for Scotland the next day, but his devotion to her makes him stay.

Moreover, because they are both devout Muslims and are not yet married, they have had little physical intimacy. Aboulela tells us "he had yet to see her hair, he had yet to know what she looks like when she cried and what she looked like when she woke up in the morning" (lines 235 – 237). However, his fascination with her is clear from the attention he pays her when they go on outings, always accompanied by other people: "he watched her how she carried a nephew, how she smiled, she peeled a grapefruit gave him a piece to eat, how she giggled with her girlfriends" (lines 249 – 251).

Because they have had so little physical contact, even in Scotland where they met, he is kept awake at night before his wedding day longing for the "comforting closeness" (line 470) which will be possible after the wedding. This results in the wonderful sensation after they are married and he sees her with her hair "long and falling on her shoulders" (line 530 – 531), wearing make-up and dressed in a red sleeveless dress. Like this she has "a secret glamour" (line 532) and "He could not stop looking at her" (line 543) and he says "God, I can't believe it" (line 534). Aboulela tells us that he cannot speak – "He was still, choked by a kind of brightness" (line 546). In the penultimate paragraph she touches his face with her hand for the very first time and this simple act is presented as a beautiful and wonderful revelation: "So that was how soft she was, that was how she smelt, that was her secret" (lines 553 – 554). Therefore, despite the tensions earlier in the story and their different cultural backgrounds, Aboulela presents this relationship in a very positive and happy light: this marriage, she seems to suggest, is going to be a success.

Note

For part (b) you might have written about 'Anil' and the ways Noor presents the father/son and mother/son relationship and how that is affected by their culture, as well as the presentation of the father's feelings as he sends Anil away. Equally, Kerry and Sandra in 'The Darkness Out there' learn a lot about Mrs Rutter, and the way their changing feelings about her are presented is interesting, as the full horror of Mrs Rutter's past becomes apparent to them.

Question 3

Part (a) Write about how the opening of 'Anil' prepares the reader for the rest of the story

The opening of 'Anil' prepares us very well for some of the later events in the story. In the opening paragraph Noor tells us that the whole village was asleep apart from one little boy who was wide awake. Everyone in the village, Noor tells us, is dreaming, but their dreams are very ordinary: they "rarely amounted to anything" (lines 3 – 4). "Housewives dreamed of tomorrow's cooking and the children dreamed of waking up to another day, and the next, and the next, until it was over as soon as it began" (lines 5 – 7). Anil, however, is immediately established as different, not simply because he is awake, but why he is awake and the way that Noor describes it. He is staring through a hole in his parents' hut at a "small star which shone down upon him" (line 14). The fact that the star is shining on Anil is important because it suggests he is different, and this prepares us, generally, for his honesty about the murder he witnesses later and also for his departure at the end of the story to the city to gain an education. The star shining down on him suggests that he is special and destined for greater things. It also shows his sensitivity: Noor tells us "His parents would not stop to gape at a star" (line 18), but Anil did because he "believed in the magical wonders of life. Because his dreams were bigger than him" (lines 19 – 20), and this too prepares us both for his courage in telling the truth about what he has seen, but also his astonishing change of fortune at the end of the story.

The opening also establishes that Anil lives in a very poor village: there are many holes in the roof of his parents' hut. We are also told that Anil, although he does not know it, is destined to be the

74

headman's servant – just as his father is now. Anil's mother is physically abused by his father: Anil can see the bruise on her shoulder where she has been hit the evening before when Anil's father came home drunk; this prepares us for the fact that women in this community are subject to violence – as we are to see with the murder and cover up of Marimuthu's wife.

Finally, Anil is also awake because his bladder is bursting and he desperately needs to go to the toilet. This reveals something important about his relationship with his parents: he does not want to wake his mother to ask to go out – because she is sleeping soundly and he is aware that his father has hit her, so Anil is established by Noor as kind and sympathetic. For the same reason, he dare not wake his father because to do so would be to risk his father's anger and the inevitable beating: "He decided that he did not need a walloping at this time of night" (line 40). This prepares us generally for the atmosphere of violence that the story contains. Because he is awake and decides to go outside on his own, Anil witnesses the murder which, together with his direct honesty, shapes the rest of the story.

Thus the opening of 'Anil' prepares us for Anil's being different and special in some way; it shows the poverty of the village and the status of women; and it gives a realistic reason for Anil to be up and about at that time of night. What we are not prepared for are the awful events that Anil witnesses and his dramatic departure at the end of the story – although the star shining down on him may, when we look back at the opening, hint at this.

Part (b) Write about how the opening of one other story from *Sunlight on the Grass* prepares the reader for the rest of the story

The first sentence of 'My Polish Teacher's Tie' reads: "I wear a uniform, blue overall and white cap with the school logo on it", in conjunction with the title itself and its possessive pronoun "my", we are initially lead to believe that the protagonist is a school pupil, when, in fact, she is a dinner lady. This is significant because one of the dominant themes in 'My Polish Teacher's Tie' is that of preconceptions and prejudice. Dunmore, effectively, tricks the reader into starting the story with their own preconceptions or assumptions

75

which she then dismantles in the second sentence: "Part-time catering staff, that's me, £3.89 per hour". We now know that Carla is, in fact, a school dinner lady.

The protagonist then describes how she "dishes out tea and buns to the teachers twice a day" and "shovel chips on the kids' trays at dinner-time". Dunmore keeps the description of Carla's work here very simple, she does not 'serve' the children she 'shovels' chips; she is part time and on a meagre wage. The reader is left with low expectations of the protagonist from the outset and the author presents a woman with a self-deprecating nature, someone who is acutely aware of her social standing. This is highlighted in line 22 and 23 where the protagonist takes ownership of the humble objects of her work: "I wrung out a cloth and wiped my surfaces". The writer is indicating that the protagonist firmly knows her place.

Carla's obvious sense of not belonging on the staff is demonstrated in line 9 the Head "sees his staff together for ten minutes once a week...". The language Dunmore uses suggests that Carla is not part of the staff and in fact feels no affiliation with them. In line 3 the omission is pertinent: "It's not a bad job. I like the kids". The protagonist suggests by omission that she does not like the staff and at line 27 her sense of inferiority and lowliness is reiterated: "Teachers are used to getting out of the way of catering staff without really seeing them". Dunmore suggests here that Carla feels invisible, excluded, which is highlighted again in line 25 when "The meeting broke up and the head vanished in a knot of teachers...." Again the collective term 'knot' suggests a sense of exclusion or inferiority; it is something which she needs to penetrate in order to reach the Head.

Having summoned up the courage to approach the Head he "stitches a nice smile on his face"; the lack of spontaneity in his response and his forced smile suggest a lack of sincerity or genuine interest. He then stumbles over the protagonist's name (line 32): "Oh, er – Mrs, er – Carter...". Having expressed an interest in the pen-friend arrangement, the Head pauses "looking at me as if it might be a trick question..." These elements again support the theme of prejudice and preconceptions which the story goes on to explore.

Returning to lines 22 and 23: "I wrung out a cloth and wiped my surfaces" - this line is highly significant because of its relationship with the title. Both the surface and the Polish Teacher are claimed by the possessive pronoun 'my', which creates interest and a compulsion to read on to discover why the lowly protagonist feels able to make a personal claim on the teacher. The readers are steered towards surmising that a relationship will evolve between the two, but the author leaves us questioning, so we have to read on to find out.

Note
With this sort of question any story from the Anthology might have been used for part (b), because in a way every story's opening prepares you in some way for what is to follow, even if the writer withholds some information. A very good choice would have been 'Something Old, Something New' because the very first paragraphs contain the man's arrival in the Sudan and his mixed reaction to being abroad as well as the meeting of the lovers at the airport, where they cannot kiss each other, and where their behaviour is inhibited by the presence of her brother as well as cultural norms. Aboulela keeps returning to these preoccupations: the Scotsman continues to feel attracted and repelled by the Sudan, and their love is circumscribed by Muslim tradition: they are never alone until after the marriage.

But others would work equally well: line 20 of 'When the Wasps Drowned' reads - 'That was the day they dug up Mr Mordechai's garden' - which is actually an event that occurs only after the end of the story and which cryptically foreshadows the whole story, while arousing the reader's interest. With 'My Polish Teacher's Tie' the simplicity of the opening paradoxically does not prepare us especially well for the complex issues of identity that the story raises. Similarly, in 'The Darkness Out There' the pleasant and innocent opening can be seen as an effective contrast with the dark events that come to light as the story progresses.

Question 4

Part (a) Write about the horrible events which Anil experiences in the story 'Anil'

You should write about:
- What Anil sees and what happens to him
- How the events make him feel
- The methods the writer uses to present the events

The horrible events in 'Anil' are central to the story and change Anil's life forever. In the middle of the night, because he is desperate to go to the toilet, Anil watches through the window of his parents' hut the murder of Marimuthu's wife, who is hanged on an old tree in the middle of the village. In the morning he tells the truth about what he sees, although the headman of the village is telling everyone that the wife of Marimuthu (who is the headman's brother) committed suicide. Fearing that Anil will reveal the truth about Marimuthu's wife's death, the headman makes a deal with Anil's father and at the end of the story Anil is effectively banished from his home village and sent completely alone to the big city, a good education and a bright future. However, for a boy so young to be wrenched from his family so suddenly and so unexpectedly is horrible. His father often used to give him a "walloping" (line 40), but, nonetheless, Noor suggests that Anil finds the separation at the end of the story upsetting and also suggests that Anil may never return through his father's words, "Remember this town" (line 207).

Anil is only seven and his age has a dramatic effect on how the events make him feel. Although Noor writes as an omniscient narrator, at crucial moments we are given Anil's direct thoughts and feelings which help convey his childish horror at what he sees. He is already frightened of the darkness of the night and having to go out alone into the dark and Noor tells us that " he dared not even think about the reason why he would not return…. as if thinking it alone was enough to bring it into being. As if they could read his mind. They. Peyi. Pesase. Ghosts" (lines 47 – 49). He then hears a noise from outside and "his eyes assumed the look of terror" (line 54 – 53). What happens next is so horrific, not only because Noor describes it from Anil's point of view, but also because events seemed to happen in slow motion and Anil slowly becomes aware of what is happening. The first thing he sees when he looks out of the window is the large ghostly tree that grew in front of the hut. Even in daytime it "looked extremely scary" (line 69). The small children of the village believe that it was a tree that eats little children, by wrapping its vines "around little kids who ventured unknowingly near it" (line 71 – 72) and then reeling the children in. He then becomes aware of something heavy being dragged on the ground, rope being thrown over one of the branches and a noose being formed. At this point we are told "his heart was beating very fast and very hard and his sweaty hands grabbed the bottom of the window" (line 81 – 82). Then he becomes aware that it wasn't a white cloth, it was a woman dressed in white; at this point "a spasm of chilling fear crept up his spine" (line 89). In the next paragraph there is worse to come: Anil realises with a shock that the woman is still alive and Anil watches her as she dies hanging from the noose. Eventually he falls asleep in the furthest corner of the hut from the window, "clutching his mouth with both hands and silencing the sobs that wracked his little body" (lines 100 – 101). Noor's deliberate and slow unfolding of Anil's realisation increases our sense of the horror about what has happened. Anil's fear of the tree returns when he wakes in the morning and sees a crowd gathered around it. He thinks, "No, don't go there" (lines 111 – 112). Anil believes that the tree has reeled in and devoured the body, and that the villagers are gathered around examining the dead woman's bones.

However, Anil shows no fear when he reveals that he saw what happened and says so to the headman. Then, at the end of the story, he faces the horrible situation of being sent away from his parents, from his home village, from everything he has ever known, and his despair is shown vividly by his thoughts as the train starts to move: "I don't want to go away. I don't want to leave you. Where am I going? How will I know you will still be here when I come back? Stop this train… stop the train!" (lines 212 – 213). Anil's sense of horror is increased as he leaves because he knows that his departure is covering up the "sin" (line 216) of the murder.

Part (b) Write about a horrible event in one other story from *Sunlight on the Grass*

You should write about:

- The event and why you think it is horrible.
- The methods the writer uses to present the event.

The most horrible event in 'When the Wasps Drowned' is the discovery of the dead body in the tunnel that Therese and Tyler are digging in a childish attempt to reach Australia. The event occurs late in the story and is hardly mentioned again: it is covered up in the same way that Eveline, the narrator, tells Therese just to fill in the tunnel. The discovery is described in a horrible way: Eveline feels the corpse's arm before she sees it and when she does she describes it in horrible detail: "The skin was mauve in places, the fingernails chipped and clogged with soil. Suddenly the day around us seemed unbearably quiet, as if everything was holding its breath" (lines 77 – 79). It is made more horrible because Wigfall has set the story in a summer of beautiful, hot weather and the children spend almost all their time playing in the garden. In such idyllic weather to discover a dead body in your next-door neighbour's garden is shocking and it is especially horrible that the discovery is made by a young child.

Eveline is haunted by the dead body's arm at night, but she tells no-one about the discovery of the body. Her sister has nightmares and Eveline comments: "When I closed my eyes I could see Therese's dream, the arm growing up through the soil" (lines 98 – 99). Only at the end of the story do the police call at the family's home and show the children a photograph of a missing girl. As readers we assume that the photo is of the dead girl in their next-door neighbour's garden, but even when questioned by the police the children, especially Eveline who is the oldest and looks after the younger two, says nothing. In this sense, Wigfall hardly presents the discovery in a central way, but her narrator has referred to it at the very beginning of the story in a single sentence paragraph which shows its importance, telling us, "That was the summer they dug up Mr Mordechai's garden" (line 20). Because Wigfall delays the discovery of the body until towards the end of the story and the visit of the police until even later, the reader does not understand the significance of that sentence: we assume that the police enquiries eventually lead them to suspect Mr Mordechai and that they dig up his garden because they think a dead body is buried there – the corpse of the missing girl. Wigfall takes great care not to tell us this part of the story: we are left to work it out for ourselves. Similarly, Wigfall leaves it to the readers' imaginations to reflect on how the girl was killed and in what way she was connected with Mr Mordechai: a horrible thing to think about or imagine. This makes the events leading to the girl's murder more mysterious and more horrible.

Because Wigfall uses a first person narrator, Eveline, there is a sense in which the events are presented through Eveline. She is an interesting narrator, and we have to question why she did not tell anyone about finding the dead body. As a character Eveline is approaching adolescence and throughout the story we are made aware of this: she is tall enough to see over the walls of their garden; she is in charge of her younger brother and sister; she notices the boys smoking at the park; she sunbathes in a home-made bikini and does not play with Therese and Tyler; interestingly she also wears the ring taken from the corpse's hand, but is careful to take it off before their mother comes home and to conceal her hand when the police call. Her taking the ring off before their mother comes home suggests a sense of guilt on her part: not about having the ring from a corpse's hand, but the wish to grow up and be an adult. She never explicitly mentions her frustration with being a child and her yearning to be an adult in the story: just like the corpse, it is covered up and remains buried. The discovery of the corpse and the police involvement is a reminder that although the adult world is full of attractions, it is also full of horrible, mysterious dangers.

Note

'The Darkness Out There' would also have been a good choice for part (b). An answer on this story might have dealt with Sandra and Kerry's reactions as they discover the truth of Mrs Rutter's actions, as well as the contrast between the descriptions of Mrs Rutter and her actions – her hypocrisy.

Question 5

Part (a) Write about the behaviour of adults in 'Anil'

You should write about:
- What the adults say and do
- The methods the writer uses to show the behaviour of the adults.

What the adults say and do in 'Anil' depends very much on their gender. Noor is writing about a patriarchal society in the developing world and the women in the story are presented as having no voice and as victims. They say and do nothing. It is made clear early on in the story that Anil's mother is physically abused by his father, and, of course, Marimuthu's wife is murdered and the crime is covered up. We never discover the name of the murdered woman: she is referred to throughout the story as Marimuthu's wife, as if that role defines her. In the morning as Anil approaches the knot of adults discussing the death he encounters first a ring of women, and then "deeper into the circle" he finds the men, closer to the tree, showing their relative importance compared with the women.

So in 'Anil' the men, especially the headman and his family, supported by his loyal henchman (Anil's own father), control everything that happens in the village and all the other adults are controlled by them. When the headman suggests that the death of Marimuthu's wife is clearly suicide, no one questions his decision, although it is interesting that "his eyes [were] darting from one face to another as he addressed the crowd" (lines 142 – 143), as if asserting his authority, but also checking that his version of events is accepted. The other adults do gossip about the possible reasons that Marimuthu's wife committed suicide, and the headman feels some embarrassment, but his real aim is to cover up the truth of the murder. Because the headman has such power and authority, he literally gets away with murder because the villagers accept what he has said:

Anil's father was one of the first to agree with the headman's decision. The rest of the villagers piped in, gesturing their agreement with the headman's wise decision (lines 144 – 145).

We never know who helped Marimuthu – whose voice it was that kept urging him on in the night: given his reaction to what Anil says, there is a strong suggestion that it may well have been the headman.

If adults behave differently because of their gender, they also behave differently in public and in private. When Anil says to Marimuthu, "You killed her. You killed your wife" (lines 159 – 160) and then says to the headman "He did it. I know he did. I saw it" (line 165), he and his father are rushed off to the headman's bungalow. Because the story is told from Anil's point of view we do not hear the discussion that occurs between the headman and Anil's father, who when he is summoned to the headman's bungalow is described as a "mouse of a man who was ever ready to serve his employer and who nodded agreeably" (line 180).

There is an abrupt break in the story to later that same day as Anil is sent off on a train to the city by his father who says "You will study hard and be an engineer, or a doctor, or a lawyer. Make this father proud of you. Do you understand?" (lines 181 – 182). In order to ensure that the truth of the murder is covered up, the headman has offered Anil the chance to be educated far away from his village. His father says to him "You are very, very lucky to have this chance" (line 182). However, our feelings and Anil's must be bitter-sweet at this lucky chance, because it all depends on keeping the truth of the murder hidden and Anil's good fortune comes as a result of the death of another human being and his father's willingness to agree to the headman's proposal.

What is striking about the end of the story, is that it reveals Anil's father's sense of shame and his guilt about helping the headman to hide the truth about Marimuthu's wife's death. This is made clear when Anil asks "Are you sending me off because I saw him do it?" (line 197). Very briefly we see his father's thoughts: "Was it wrong that he sacrificed the truth and justice for his son's only chance out of an otherwise dreary life like his" (lines 201 – 202). The end of the story shows both father and son in tears: Anil because he is leaving all that is familiar to him and he has no idea when he will see his parents again; Ragunathan because he is letting his only son leave, but also because he is ashamed of his subservience to the headman and his willing acquiescence in covering up a terrible crime. The final section serves to demonstrate that despite his violence and illiteracy, Ragunathan is aware of his faults: Anil saw him fall to his knees "a bent, despaired figure" (line 214).

The final line of the story reminds us of the corruption in the village and the power of the headman and his family: as the headman has the "shadow of a smile on his lips" (line 225) and they watch the train taking Anil away, Marimuthu "heaved a sigh of relief" (line 226). This chilling ending shows the power that some adults have in this story.

Part (b) Write about the behaviour of adults or an adult in one other story from *Sunlight on the Grass*

You should write about:

- What the adult or adults say and do
- The methods the writer uses to show this behaviour.

In 'Compass and Torch' Baines adopts an omniscient narrative position. The paragraph commencing at line 19 which details the overheard monologue of the boy's mother is particularly revealing. The mother is shown to express an array of emotions, all resulting from the prospect of the forthcoming camping trip. Her disdain and angst are unequivocal: "Mad! The first time in four months he has his eight-year-old son and what does he plan to do? Take him camping up a mountain! Talk about macho avoidance activity!" Baines describes Jim's response as "an unhappy kind of rustle" (line 23). We can assume from this that the new boyfriend feels uncomfortable with the mother's outburst but wishes to remain neutral. The paragraph ends with the mother asking the rhetorical question: "Well, what do you expect?" She clearly does not anticipate or require a response as the paragraph closes with: "There was a kind of choke in her voice now, and suddenly a kind of snarl: 'You wouldn't expect him to start now, would you – accommodating his child into his life?'" All this is overheard by the boy and the mother, who, attempting to compensate for her words, somewhat inadequately 'wrenches' a look of bright enthusiasm onto her face (line 29). Baines' choice of the word 'wrench' suggests that the mother's countenance is grossly at odds with her inner feelings.

When describing Jim's interaction with the boy the author repeats variations of the word 'kind', first at line 31: "Jim asked kindly, 'Is it all in working order?'' and again at line 35: "'Yes,' said the boy, forcing himself to acknowledge Jim's kindness and affirmation." We can assume from this, together with Jim's silence during the mother's monologue, that he is a good-natured man who wishes to remain impartial.

The paragraph beginning at line 103 reveals more of the adults' strained dynamics and their rather unsuccessful attempts to normalise the situation for the boy. The boy sees through the charade though: "...he couldn't wait to get going, for it all to be over: the way his dad said 'Hi there!' In that brittle, jovial way to Jim, and the way Jim dropped his eyes when he'd said 'Hi' back, as if he understood all there was to understand about Dad..." It is clear from the boy's observations of these social nuances that he is very aware of the tension between the adults.

In the same paragraph the mother is shown to be incapable of concealing her sentiments, Baines writes : "And the way his mother said hardly anything, and made her face blank whenever Dad spoke to her or looked her way, and kept shredding a tissue so bits leaked through her fingers to the floor." (line 108) Similarly, at line 111: "she put her head in through the car window, and her eyes were bulging and wobbly with tears..." The adults' combined behaviour and their attempts to conceal the stresses from the boy are shown to be futile as the author writes at line 117: "And then the worst thing of all: that brief but really awful moment when the car slid out of the drive and he felt, after all, he didn't want to go." Their actions have served only to disenchant the child.

In 'Compass and Torch' the adults are compelled to conceal emotions, however, unbeknown to them, the child is acutely aware of all the strains of an altered family dynamic. As the reader we know that the dialogue between the parties should be open and honest. However, we are only able to mutely witness the collapse of the relationship. As the story closes, the father, totally oblivious to his son's devotion, concedes defeat (line 166): "He could feel it gathering in the blackening chill: the aching certainty that already, only one year on from the separation, he has lost his son, his child" (line 166). Knowing of the boy's devotion and his strong will to sustain their relationship, the father's defeatist conclusion creates a great sense of frustration.

Note

For part (b) 'My Polish Teacher's Tie' would also have been a good choice: you might have written about the contrast between the way Carla behaves at school and the way she behaves at home. 'The Darkness Out There' would also have given you a lot to write about, focusing on the behaviour of Mrs Rutter now and in the past.

Question 6

Part (a) Write about the ways Lively presents an unpleasant experience in 'The Darkness Out There'

Lively's story opens with the innocuous line: "She walked through the flowers, the girl, ox-eye daisies and vetch and cow parsley..." It then goes on to talk about the Good Neighbour's Club, the 'nice' old folks and the protagonist's sweet and simple dreams : "She would go to places in travel brochures and run into a blue sea. She would fall in love..." (line 66). The combined effect evokes the essence of a safe and friendly world. However, the story quickly turns to 'Packer's End' and the imagined and real dangers contained within. Together with the title, 'The Darkness Out There', the reader is left with a sense of foreboding.

The author uses the same devices when the story turns to the events at the old lady's house. She describes Mrs Rutter as having a "creamy smiling pool of a face..." However, the sentence ends with: "...in which her eyes snapped and darted..." (line 96). In effect the first part of the sentence creates an inviting persona, while the latter part suggests a more unpleasant nature. Similarly, within her house, the author describes the physical features of the cottage : "...big-eyed flop-eared rabbits and beribboned kittens and flowery milkmaids and a pair of naked chubby children wearing daisy chains" (line 102). The objects which the woman has surrounded herself with suggest a sentimental, kindly and somewhat old-fashioned person. The home becomes an inviting place. But, within the same paragraph Lively also mentions that there is a "smell of cabbage", something which children commonly find repugnant. The conflicting details, together with the title and the introduction of the real and imagined horrors of Packer's End, prepare the reader for a more sinister development.

As the story evolves and the children engage in conversation with Mrs Rutter, her true nature becomes more apparent. She purports to value the quality of 'niceness' in other people (lines 151, 158 and 161: 'That's a nice boy', 'ever such a nice person' and 'He was a lovely man'). However, her response to Kerry's plans for the future lack sensitivity : "Well, I expect that's good steady money if you'd nothing special in mind" (line 114). In effect, Lively has Mrs Rutter assume that the job at the garage is 'nothing special' to Kerry but it could equally be the realisation of his lifetime ambition.

When Mrs Rutter discloses her activities on the night the aircraft came down Sandra is described variously as shuddering, crying, grimacing and stiffening (lines 273, 292, 296 and 304) whilst Kerry's outrage manifests itself in expletive: "Christ!" (line 347) and "I'm not going near that old bitch again" (line 352). The children's fury and revulsion heighten the horror of the woman's inaction, but what highlights the dreadful inaction most starkly is that Lively's Mrs Rutter claims to like young people : "I've got sympathy with young people" (line 342). She divulges this after having told the children that the surviving airman was so badly injured that she had been unable to decipher how old he was : "I'd thought he was an old bloke, too, but he wasn't. He'd have been twentyish, that sort of age"(line 321). We can assume from information the author has provided that Kerry is very near to this age which again serves to amplify the horror of the experience and the woman's callous disregard for the dying man.

And then part (b) Write about how the writer presents an unpleasant experience in one other story from *Sunlight on the Grass*

In 'When the Wasps Drowned' Clare Wigfall presents Therese getting stung by the wasps as an unpleasant experience, but one which has no lasting effects, although she draws attention to it by naming the story after the event. The title and the opening sentence refer to Therese's experience as the narrator, Eveline, tells us, "That was the summer Therese stepped on the wasps' nest and brought an end to our barefoot wanderings" (lines 1 – 2). This suggests that the experience, as well as the prolonged good weather, is the narrator's defining memory of that particular summer: but this is Wigfall's skill as a writer because by the end of the story we know that a very different experience or event is actually the abiding memory of that summer.

After the opening sentence, the narrator only returns to the wasps in the fifth paragraph and slowly leads the reader up to the actual experience. "We heard her screams from inside," Eveline tells us in line 21 and it was so shocking to her that she dropped a glass while doing the washing up. Therese's screaming was so loud that "it broke the day" (24 – 25) and we see what Eveline saw; "She was running in circles round the garden, shrieking, a halo of angry wasps blurring her shape, her pigtails dancing" (lines 26 – 27). This is an unusual image because although Therese is obviously in pain and the wasps are angry, halos are associated with very saintly or religious images, so they have very positive connotations and in addition the pigtails are dancing. Perhaps this suggests that, although being stung by so many wasps is extremely unpleasant, it does not cause lasting damage and compared with the later discovery of the corpse beneath the wall: it is merely unpleasant not horrific and disturbing. Indeed, Tyler laughed when Eveline turned the hose on Therese: "he thought it was all a joke" (line 31). Although Therese continued "to scream into the afternoon" (lines 32 – 33), Eveline says that her dress clung to her like "a polka dot of red welts" (line 32 : another image which mixes the unpleasant red welts with a word that has much happier associations – polka dot).

As the summer progresses we are reminded of the incident with the wasps: when they walk to the park Therese is picking at her scabs. However, while Eveline sunbathes in the garden, Therese scoured the grass for wasp corpses and takes her revenge by crushing their bodies to dust with stones. Wigfall uses the wasp incident as a way of foreshadowing and putting into perspective the appalling discovery of the murdered girl in the tunnel that Therese and Tyler are using to dig to Australia. Significantly, it is only after the discovery of the corpse that Therese starts to have bad dreams: Eveline overhears her voice explaining her dream to their mother: "I was watering the garden, Mum, with the blue watering can, and it started to grow" (line2 96 - 97), clearly referring to the dead girl's hand. She does not have bad dreams about the wasps: the children in the story are presented as being able to overcome wasp stings, but the effect of finding a corpse in their neighbour's garden is far more disturbing, and one they would rather ignore and deny all knowledge of.

Note

The other story from the Anthology which would have been an excellent choice to write about is 'Anil', because it gives you so much to write about: Anil's desperation to go to the toilet and his fear of the ghosts outside; his mistreatment by his father; the murder; the cover up of the murder; and his being packed off to a distant school at the end of the story. 'Anil' gives you a lot to write about in terms of Noor's technique too, because Anil's fears – which begin with a generalized fear of the darkness of the night are slowly and progressively built up by Noor into Anil's shocking witness of the murder.

Question 7

Part (a) Write about how Dunmore presents Carla, the narrator, in 'My Polish Teacher's Tie

Carla is presented as someone acutely aware of her self-perceived social standing and her position in staff hierarchy. In the first paragraph the protagonist describes herself purely in terms of her working position and she does this with emphasis on all the more negative traits of her role: her lowly wage, the part time nature of her position, even through to the language she uses to describe serving food : "Part-time catering staff, that's me, £3.89 per hour. I dish out tea and buns to the teachers twice a day and shovel chips on to the kids' trays at dinner-time." The choice of 'shovel' and 'dish' rather than 'serve' stresses that this is not a high-end catering establishment, merely a perfunctory school canteen.

Carla recognises herself as an entirely separate entity to the teaching staff. Dunmore describes how the dinner lady "wipe(s) my surfaces" (line23), the possessive 'my' suggests that she accepts her lesser role and at line 100 the protagonist explicitly states her position: "Colleagues don't wear blue overalls and white caps and work for £3.89 an hour." Carla is presented as someone who, while mindful of her position, has a propensity, through her inadequacies, to collectivise and dismiss the teaching staff. She generalises in line 27: "Teachers are used to getting out of the way of catering staff without really seeing them."

Having established that Carla recognises herself as a separate and lesser entity to the teachers, line 8 betrays a more sarcastic side to the protagonist. In divulging the teachers' kitty for entitlement to tea and buns, she says: "...Very keen on fairness, we are, here." It is clear that she does not consider herself part of the 'we' she describes and herein lies the sarcasm.

We learn through the story that Carla is a parent, probably a single parent. No reference is made to a partner or husband, but at times her rationale appears child-like. In line 53 she belligerently states: "I didn't write anything about my job. Let him think what he wanted to think. I wasn't lying". Similarly, in line 62 Dunmore has the protagonist confess that: "I used to write a bit every day then make myself wait until the middle of the week to send it." Both echo a child-like mentality.

Despite this Dunmore also presents Carla as an accurate but silent observer of human traits (line 78): "...said the head raising his voice the way he does so that one minute he's talking to you and the next it's a public announcement." Again, at line 117 Dunmore highlights how Carla is acutely way of the mannerisms of those around her: "...Always holding up the queue saying she's on a diet, and then taking the biggest bun." After she sees Steve, this observational side of her takes on an empathetic slant. Dunmore writes (line 142): "He was sitting stiffly upright, smiling in the way people smile when they don't quite understand what's going on" (line 142). She continues: "The Head was wagging a sheaf of papers in front of him, and talking very loudly as if he was deaf."

Finally, after having plucked up the courage to introduce herself to Steve, the protagonist is shown to embrace her love of poetry and language which, without Steve, she feels unable to embrace as demonstrated at line 121: "And then there was the poetry book I'd bought. It seemed a shame to bin it. It might come in use for Jade. I thought." Having met Steve, Dunmore introduces metaphor and analogy into Carla's language (line 156): "Tense as a guitar string" and (line 165): "It went through me like a knife through butter" (line 165). Finally, the protagonist concludes with a fresh confidence: "His red tie with its bold green squiggles was much too wide and much too bright. It was a flag from another country, a better country than the ones either of us lived in." Her final observations suggest a much richer and more sentient character than the story originally reveals.

Part (b) How does the writer present the narrator of one other story from *Sunlight on the Grass?*

The narrator of 'On Seeing the 100% Perfect Girl One Beautiful Spring Morning' is presented in an interesting way, because we know so little about him, even though Murakami uses him as the narrator, and because the story he tells is so unusual and rather timeless – it has elements reminiscent of fairy tales, but is set in modern Tokyo, with references to the very popular Harajuki district. His tone as narrator is at once self-deprecatory and very serious, so his story veers between poking fun at himself and how ridiculous he is, and a rather touching romantic yearning to fall in love with the 100% perfect girl of the title. He seems to believe in the possibility of perfect love, while at the same time mocking himself for doing so, for keeping faith in a romantic, optimistic view of relationships. This tension between his ideal and the down-to-earth reality of his life makes the story funny – in a very gentle, wistful, slightly melancholic way.

The narrator establishes a close relationship with the reader by directly addressing us, by using the present tense, which gives an immediacy to his style, and by the honesty of what he tells us. Having told us that he has seen the 100% perfect girl he admits "tell you the truth, she's not that good looking. She doesn't stand out in any way" (line 3). However he asserts that "I know from 50 yards away: she is the 100% perfect girl for me" (line 6). This slightly ridiculous scenario suggests that the narrator is very lonely and is desperate to meet the 100% perfect girl. He admits to the reader:

maybe you have your own particular favourite type of girl – one with slim ankles, say, or big eyes, or graceful fingers, or you're drawn for no good reason to girls who take their time with every meal (lines 9 – 12).

This is amusing because some of these characteristics are so random and so trivial that they seem a poor foundation for a lasting relationship. The narrator admits that "sometimes in a restaurant I catch myself staring at the girl at the table next to mine because I like the shape of her nose" (lines 12 – 13), but he admits as far as the 100% perfect girl he has seen: "I can't recall the shape of hers – or even if she had one" (line15). This brief image of a possibly nose-less woman is amusing and weird.

Of course, it would be even more weird to address a complete stranger on the street and the way he imagines the different things that he might have said to her is doubly amusing, because in the event he says nothing and when he turns to look at her she is lost in the crowd. It is clear that the narrator is partly living in a dream world: "Wish I could talk to her. Half an hour would be plenty" (line 28). As she gets closer he becomes more anxious: "How can I approach her? What should I say?" (line 37). He rejects the idea of asking her to spend half an hour for a conversation or asking her whether she knows if there are any all-night cleaners in the area: he dismisses these ideas as ridiculous. He considers telling her the simple truth: "Good morning. You are the 100% perfect girl for me" (lines 45 – 46). Interestingly he doesn't do this, not because it would be ridiculous or weird to say this to a complete stranger, so he says, but in case she rejects him.

The story that he then tells, which begins "Once upon a time there lived a boy and a girl" (line 64), is, he decides, what he should have said to the 100% perfect girl that he saw at random on the street. The story itself is about how he and the 100% perfect girl met and fell in love when they were younger, but how as the years passed and adulthood and maturity dominated their lives, they forgot about one another and, although they become "truly upstanding citizens who knew how to transfer from one subway line to another, who were fully capable of sending a special delivery letter at the post office" (lines 100 – 102), they lose the ability to love 100% and when they do pass each other on the street (as they have done at the start of Murakami's story), "the glow of their memories was far too weak, and their thoughts no longer had the clarity of fourteen years earlier" (lines 113 – 114). Without a word, they passed each other, disappearing into the crowd for ever.

The narrator of this story is a lonely 32-year-old man who yearns to rediscover the innocence and passion of youth and who perhaps naïvely believes, against all the odds, that somewhere for him is the 100% perfect girl. At the end of his fantasy story, he declares "Yes that's it, that is what I should have said to her" (line 117): as if this romantic but sad story, told to a complete stranger, would have been any less ridiculous than asking the whereabouts of an all-night cleaners.

Note

The other story that could have been used for part (b) is 'When the Wasps Drowned', because of the calm way Eveline describes the horrific events of that long, hot summer. The fact that her calmness might also be seen as a deliberate attempt not to think about all the things in her life that are changing would have given you a lot to write about. The same could be said for the matter-of-fact way in which the killing of the wasps is described. Another good focus would have been on the behaviour of Mrs Rutter and/or Sandra in 'The Darkness Out There', focusing on what they say and do. Lively also presents Mrs Rutter in an interesting way, and she uses structure and language to contrast how Mrs Rutter is now compared with how she was in the past.

Question 8

Answer **part (a)** and **part (b)**

Part (a)

Writes about how Baines presents the boy in 'Compass and Torch'.

In 'Compass and Torch' Baines never mentions the boy's Christian name, he is simply referred to as 'the boy'. This means that while we can relate to the boy's oscillating emotions we are partly estranged from the character without the familiarity of a name, this mirrors the theme of estrangement or the potential estrangement of father and son. The child is in a vulnerable place emotionally and Baines' choice of location, a wilderness in which hostile sounding 'ancient rocks glint like heaving carcasses' (line 80) and 'ghost-coloured ponies' (line 146) roam, serves to highlight his defencelessness.

Stylistically the story is told through the voice of the omniscient narrator, which adds to the readers' sense of alienation from the child; we can only observe from the distance this allows as the story unfolds.

The boy is clearly devoted to his father, to the point of hero-worship, and Baines uses repetition to stress this: 'The boy is intent. Watching Dad. Watching what Dad is. Drinking it in: the essence of Dadness'(line8). This repetition also suggests that the boy is trying to memorise the moment, such is its importance to him. When they encounter the horse who 'provides a close up display which could easily fascinate an eight-year-old-boy' ('opens and flexes her bright red arse and lets out a steaming stream (line 133)') the boy remains focused on his father almost to the point that he is blind to his immediate surroundings:

Unseen by the man and boy, clouds sweep like opening curtains above the brow of the hill and the grass lights up, bright yellow. Ancient rocks glint like heaving carcasses asleep (line 78).

Similarly, on line 147, the pair, on reaching the peak: '...do not stop, as most walkers do, to take in the view, the purple sweep of the plain towards the blue wall of mountains beyond. They keep going...'

Both father and son are consumed with one another to the exclusion of all else.

The boy in Baines' story is presented as a watchful, anxious child. Keen to please both his parents but equally torn by them, he is acutely aware of their mannerisms and the intonation in their voices. Baines writes on line 24: 'There was a choke in her voice now, and suddenly a kind of snarl...' Similarly, on line 90 when the man groans, saying: 'I didn't bring a compass':

The boy's eyes are suddenly wide with fear and dismay: not with the notion that they'll get lost, but because of the way the man's shoulder slumped and the tent in his hand dropped back onto the boot floor.

The strain on his parental allegiance is confirmed as the boy reflects on the events responsible for him leaving his compass behind:

And then the worst thing of all: that brief but really awful moment when the car slid out of the drive and he felt, after all, that he didn't want to go. That was another reason the compass never entered his head (line 117).

The boy's interaction with his mother's boyfriend increases the sense of a brittle tension in family life. Baines repeats permutations of 'forced' in her description of their contact. On line 32 the author writes: 'The boy forced himself to put the torch into Jim's big-outstretched hand, to stand still and attentive...'It's a good one,' said Jim...'Yes,' said the boy, forcing himself to acknowledge Jim's kindness...' It is clear that the boy is resistant to this relationship and while aware of Jim's kindness, he hankers for the way things used to be.

On the camping trip Baines pivots the conversation between father and son on the compass, torch and tent. They do not discuss mutual anxieties and internalize their various thoughts and feelings. That the conversation revolves around these inanimate objects suggests that the boy is trying to establish common ground, mutual likes and at a deeper level an enduring bond between them both. On line 135 the Baines writes: "Is it the kind of compass where the top lifts up, like mine?', asks the boy eagerly, with eyes only for the man.'

As the story prepares to close the boy continues 'gabbling' until he has 'chattered himself out' (line 170) but we know that the chatter is not sparked by excitement but by fear, it is almost as if the boy is trying to cram words into the limited time he has with his father and the author confirms this when he writes on the father's mutual fears: 'He could feel it gathering in the blackening chill: the aching certainty that already, only one year on...he had lost his son, his child. And the thought grew so strong that he could only half listen to the child's earnest desperate voice' (line 166). Yet, despite the child's clear devotion, the adult fails to take the opportunity afforded him by the trip to reassure his son.

and then **part (b)**

How does the writer present the young person in **one** other story from *Sunlight on the Grass*?

'Anil' by Ridjal Noor presents Anil is a frightened and vulnerable victim of the corrupt village that he lives in, and the tyrannical rule of the village Headman. Anil is also physically and verbally abused by his own father. However, Noor presents Anil as also having qualities of courage and intelligence – which get him into more trouble.

Noor expertly and very gradually builds up Anil's fear at the start of the story. At the start of the story Anil's mundane need is to leave the hut because his bladder is bursting; he decides not to wake his father up so that he can accompany him because 'he did not need a walloping at this time of the night' (line 40). But he is afraid of the dark and the ghosts whom he believes may capture a small boy such as him.

He is then alerted by a sound from outside the hut and, in his childish imagination, he assumes it is a ghost or some spirit of the night. His fear is vividly conveyed by Noor:

His eyes assumed the look of terror. Suspended into suspense. Expecting a ghastly face to emerge at the window and send him screaming his head off, yet he could not bring himself to look away from the window. If there was something out there, he wanted to be prepared for it. (lines 53 – 57)

Noor also reveals that Anil and the other children of the village are terrified of a large, ghostly tree that was in front of his hut, believing that 'It was a tree that ate little children' (line 73). However, the evil that Anil then witnesses has a very human side to it. He watches in horror as two men (one of whom he recognizes as Marimuthu, the brother of the village headman) who are engaged in hanging from a noose the dead body of a woman up into the branches of the tree. Anil's fear is clear: his 'little body trembled for a moment, as a spasm of chilling fear crept up his spine' (lines 88 -89). But his horror increases as he realizes that the woman is, in fact, still alive and he has to watch her death throes as she is strangled by the noose: 'Anil watched, numb with the horror' (lines 94 – 95). He is so shocked and horrified by what he has witnessed that he crouches in a corner of the hut for the rest of the night, sleeping only fitfully – 'A little boy, clutching his mouth with both hands and silencing the sobs that wracked his little body' (lines 100 – 101).

But Anil is much more than a helpless victim of the violence that surrounds him and Noor's writing has prepared us for this. At the very start of the story Noor suggested through his writing that Anil possessed qualities that mark him out as different and superior to his fellow villagers. As he lies awake in the family hut, his bladder bursting, he gazes at a star which he can see through the hole in the roof of the hut. What is significant is what Noor says about Anil's gazing at the star:

He found the star fascinating. His parents would not even stop for a second to gape at a star. But he did. Because he believed in the magical wonders of life. Because his dreams were bigger than him. (lines 17 – 20)

Anil is very frightened by what he sees happening at the twisted tree, but he perseveres in watching, and the following morning, as the villagers gather around the tree to gossip about the death of Marimuthu's wife – which the headman is trying to pretend was suicide, it is Anil, despite his age, despite his fear, despite his status as a victim, who has the honesty and courage to say quite openly to Marimuthu: "You killed her. You killed your wife" (lines 159 – 160) and then says to the headman "He did it. I know he did. I saw it" (line 165).

This very public accusation of Marimuthu leads to the headman effectively exiling Anil from his home village, by agreeing with Anil's father to send him to the city to be privately educated. Anil's father can see that this solution offers his son a route out of the poverty of village life, but Anil's leave-taking causes him more suffering. Even his usually brutal father is distraught at letting his son go, knowing he will not see him for many years. Anil's long-term future is bright: his father encourages him by saying, 'You are going to be studying in a big university and becoming someone great one day' (lines 183 – 184), but even he at the end of the story is 'a bent, despaired figure' on his knees as Anil's train recedes into the distance.

The ending of the story displays Anil's intelligence: he is well aware of why he is being sent away and asks his father, 'Are you sending me off because I saw him do it?' (line 197). But the overwhelming impression Noor gives us of Anil at the end of the story is of a small boy who is frightened of what the future holds. Noor even gives us a direct insight into Anil's thoughts: 'I don't want to go away. I don't want to leave you. Where am I going? How will I know you'll still be here when I come back? Stop the train…stop the train!' (lines 212 – 213). Despite Anil's honesty, intelligence and courage, he is presented throughout the story as a frightened victim – of ghosts and child-eating trees at the start of the story and of the very real evil corruption of his village's headman at the end of the story.

Note

We have used 'Anil' to answer part (b), but the change in Kerry in 'The Darkness Out There' would have also made a good basis for a response. Equally, Eveline in 'When the Wasps Drowned', especially as she is the narrator of the story, would have been a good character to choose to answer this part of the question.

Question 9

Answer **part (a)** and **part (b)**

Part (a)

How does the writer present feelings in 'On Seeing the 100% Perfect Girl One Beautiful April Morning'?

One of the most important things to notice about the presentation of feelings in this story is that they are completely central: indeed, the young man who narrates the story tells us only about his feelings for the perfect girl that he passed in the streets that morning. We know nothing about his work, his living arrangements, his hobbies and pastimes, or even his name – the entire story is focused on the feelings that he has about the perfect girl and the thoughts that she provokes.

In the opening of the story, which is written in the present tense to give it more immediacy and in which the narrator addresses the reader very casually in a matey, blokey way, the feelings that he has are clearly motivated by sexual attraction – although with a clear emphasis on fantasy or day-dreaming. He imagines that once he has spoken to her, 'we'd have lunch somewhere, maybe see a Woody Allen movie, stop by a hotel bar for cocktails. With any kind of luck, we might end up in bed' (lines 33 – 34). So he is clearly motivated by sexual desire. However, because he cannot think of any way of starting a conversation which will not be seen as ridiculous, his brief daydream is irrelevant: they pass without exchanging a word and soon she is lost in the crowd. It is clear that the narrator is disturbed and anxious because he can think of no way to start a conversation: 'In fact, even from fifty yards away she provokes 'a rumbling in my chest, and my mouth is as dry as a desert' (lines 7 – 8).

Prior to this, in conversation with a vague 'someone' (line 17) and in his remarks to the reader, the narrator has placed great emphasis on the qualities that might be a part of someone's 'perfect girl' and all the characteristics mentioned are physical ones: 'slim ankles', 'big eyes', 'graceful fingers', 'the shape of her eyes or the size of her breasts'. This concentration on the purely physical aspects of a woman's appearance may be typical of some men and can be quite offensive to women, since it pays no attention to their personality or character: it turns women into objects of male desire. In the first two pages of the story the only things which make this more than a day-dream of lust are his description of her as the 100% perfect girl, his anxiety about speaking to her and his amused self-awareness that even if he says, 'Good morning. You are the 100% perfect girl for me' (lines 45 – 46), she might well reply, 'Sorry… but you're not the 100% perfect boy for me' (lines 48 -49). The first two sides have a comic feel: there is the parody of male attitudes to women – reducing them to 'thin ankles'; the ridiculous idea of being able to tell that a woman is the 100% perfect girl from fifty yards away; even the idea of approaching a complete stranger on the street to tell her she is the 100% perfect girl. So we can say the feelings are not presented seriously by Murakami: he even allows the narrator an awareness of how ridiculous he is being.

The narrator then proceeds to tell us what he should have said to the girl he passed in the street, and he then launches into a version of how his life and the girl's might have been different had they met earlier in life and the feelings – while still retaining a strong element of fantasy – become much more serious in their presentation, because Murakami is making a serious point about what happens as we grow older and lose our youthful innocence.

The change in the story is marked by a change to the past tense and Murakami begins with the words 'Once upon a time' (line 64) which makes what follows have a fairy tale element. The pair meet and speak honestly with each other: they admit quite openly that they are 100% right for each other and spend hours talking and holding hands. Murakami comments, 'What a wonderful thing it is to find and be found by your 100% perfect other. It's a cosmic miracle' (lines 77 - 78). But the pair agree to go their separate ways – confident that if they are such perfect matches for each other, then they are bound to meet again in the future. The narrator ruefully comments that the test they had agreed on was 'utterly unnecessary' (line 88) and that they are so perfect together they should never have parted. In this section feelings have been presented in an idyllic way and central to what it means for human beings to be happy and fulfilled.

One winter they both catch influenza and their memories are erased. Nonetheless, they grow up and become what Murakami calls 'fully-fledged members of society' (line 99). One day, many years later, when the boy is a man of 32 and the girl is a woman of 30, they pass in the street and. although there is some glow of a memory in both of them, the adult world has changed them and they pass each other without acknowledging the other…forever.

Murakami presents feelings as absolutely central to what it means to be human and to feel happy and fulfilled. He also seems to suggest in his presentation of feelings that growing older and becoming adults affects our ability to love 100%, and this provokes a sense of loss and sadness. He says of the two young people, as they grow up, that 'they even experienced love again, sometimes as much as 75% or 85%' (lines 103 – 104), but never 100% again. In this sense, Murakami or his narrator sees the process of becoming an adult as one which diminishes our capacity to love fully and wholeheartedly, and which means we will never be able to re-capture the innocence and whole-hearted enthusiasm of our youthful feelings of total commitment and faith in the ones we choose to love.

and then **part (b)**

Write about how feelings are presented in **one** other story from *Sunlight on the Grass*.

In 'My Polish Teacher's Tie' the protagonist, Carla Carter, addresses the reader directly in the first person narrative. This allows us an insight into the characters innermost thoughts and feelings. The story begins with: 'I wear a uniform, blue overall and white cap with the school logo on it. Part-time catering staff, that's me, £3.89 per hour.' Instantly we get a sense of lowliness about the character, the author having chosen to reveal Carla's meagre wage and humble job at the outset, almost as if these details define her. Carla continues on line three with: 'It's not a bad job. I like the kids.' By omission the character reveals that she does not like the teaching staff and this is confirmed when she employs sarcasm to describe the teacher's tea and bun scheme:

The teachers pay for their tea and buns. It's one of those schemes teachers are good at. So much in a kitty, and that entitles them to cups of tea and buns for the rest of the term. Visitors pay, too, or it wouldn't be fair. Very keen on fairness, we are, here (line 5).

The sarcastic use of 'we' indicates a degree of resentment on the character's part. Clearly she does not perceive herself as being part of the 'we' she describes and in taking ownership of her surfaces at line 23, her sense of inadequacy or lowliness is cemented: 'I wrung out a cloth and wiped my surfaces.'

The protagonist's sense of exclusion amongst the school staff is reaffirmed at line 25 with the impenetrable collective description used to describe the teachers: 'The Head vanished in a knot of teachers…' Similarly on line 26 the character remarks: 'Teachers are used to getting out of the way of catering staff without really seeing them.' This suggests that Carla feels invisible and on line 100 the character's perceived sense of exclusion is confirmed: 'Colleagues don't wear blue overalls and white caps and work for £3.89 an hour.' She clearly does not feel part of the school's fraternity.

When Carla approaches the head he 'stitches a nice smile on his face', the use of the word 'stitching' in association with human flesh creates a painful visual image and indicates a reluctance on the Head's part to converse with the dinner lady. He then stumbles over her name at line 32: 'Oh, er – Mrs, er – Carter. Is there a problem?' This hesitancy affirms the character's sense of exclusion, the Head appears to be unfamiliar with her.

When Carla engages in letter exchanges with the Polish teacher, Steve, the writer reveals that she has possessive feelings. When Jade asks her mother about the letter on line 46, the protagonist is evasive: 'Just a letter. You can have the stamp if you want.' She responds similarly when the Head asks her whether she ever wrote to the teacher: ''Yes,' I said. Nothing more. Let him think I'd written once then not bothered….(line 76).' Both instances suggest that Carla wants to keep the correspondence private, for her eyes only.

After the story reveals that Steve is coming to England Carla's sense of inadequacy manifests again. She has failed to reveal her true role within the school and has let Steve assume that she too is teaching staff. Without this guise her feelings of worthlessness resurface: 'But what was worse was that he was going to expect to meet me. Or not me, exactly, but the person he'd been writing too, who didn't really exist (line 96).' The extent or her personal inadequacy means that despite her re-kindled love of poetry, with thoughts of Steve's rejection, she no longer feels worthy to pursue her interest (line 121): 'And then there was the poetry book I'd bought. It seemed a shame to bin it. It might come in use for Jade, I thought.' Without Steve she feels unqualified to sustain her pursuit of poetry.

When Carla finally meets Steve, Dunmore introduces metaphor and simile into Carla's words, a change which correlates with Carla's heightened emotions. The protagonist's more inventive use of language reveals a growing confidence, qualified by her connection with Steve. On line 165 the protagonist describes how Steve's song went through her 'like a knife through butter' and on line 174 she describes Steve's tie as a 'flag from another country…' The inventive imagery reveals the character's happiness and jubilation; despite her worst fears Steve has accepted her for who she is.

Note

The man's confused and mixed feelings in 'Something Old, Something New' would give you a great deal to write about in the area of feelings in his ambivalent responses to Sudan and Islamic culture. In 'When the Wasps Drowned' Eveline's feelings are often repressed or hidden, but Wigfall uses dreams to show us her horror at the discovery of the dead girl buried in the garden. In 'Compass and Torch' as well the feelings of the man and his son are expressed cleverly but indirectly through their dialogue and actions.

Question 10

Part (a)

Write about family life in 'Compass and Torch'.

You should write about:

- what the people in the family say and do

- the methods the writer uses to show family life.

From the omniscient narrative it is clear that family life in Compass and Torch is complex and strained. The mother and father have been separated for a year and the mother now lives with her new boyfriend, Jim and the boy. The mother feels bitter animosity towards the father, this is revealed in the dialogue between herself and Jim:

Mad, she was calling it, as he knew she would. 'Mad! The first time in four months he has his eight-year-old son and what does he plan to do? Take him camping up a mountain! Talk about macho avoidance activity! (line 19).

Later, the boy recounts overhearing his mother and her vitriol is unequivocal:

No hope of him relating to his son on any personal, day-to-day level! No hope of him trying to RELATE to him, full stop! (line 101).

Jim, on the other hand, is presented as an individual eager to bond with the boy but uncomfortable being party to the mother's disdain towards the father. Baines talks about Jim 'shifting at the kitchen table with an unhappy kind of rustle' (line 23). His discomfort suggests that he wishes to remain neutral and what the boy interprets as hatred towards his father is more likely to be shame or pity, this is indicated in Jim's response to the father's greeting: 'Jim dropped his eyes when he'd said Hi back...' (line 105). Little time has elapsed since the father left and Jim moved in, which suggests that Jim might have been instrumental in the separation.

The boy is polite towards Jim but his interaction is strained, when Jim asks about the boy's torch 'The boy forced himself to put the torch in Jim's big out-stretched hand' (line 32) and when Jim comments that it's a good torch the author again uses permutations of the word 'force': 'Yes, said the boy, forcing himself to acknowledge Jim's kindness and affirmation' (line 35). However, the boy's anger later turns to both his mother and Jim, despite Jim having remained silent on the matter of the boy's father. He clearly sees his mother and Jim as a couple and harbours no illusions that the separation is temporary: "Now you will be careful? Don't go camping too near the edge.' Unforgiveable – as if she and Jim didn't think that Dad could think of such a thing himself' (line 115). While the mother verbalises the warning, the boy perceives it as a statement coming from both herself and Jim.

While the boy is protective of his father he is clearly torn between his parents. Baines writes: '…her eyes were bulging and wobbly with tears, and he thought he couldn't bear this: that she didn't want him to go, that this moment which he had looked forward to, longed for, as his moment of joy, was a moment of unhappiness for her' (line 114). The boy clearly wishes to please both parents but the situation puts him in an impossible situation, one that would be particularly difficult for an eight-year-old to comprehend.

The boy is devoted to his father, this is apparent in the repetition of 'Dad' on line 8: 'The boy is intent. Watching Dad. Watching what Dad is. Drinking it in: the essence of Dadness.' His adoration is so strong that while on the expedition with his father his attention is focused solely on his father to the exclusion of anything else. When the horse provides a 'close up display which could easily fascinate an eight-year-old boy: opens and flexes her bright-red arse and lets out a steaming stream' (line 132) the boy's attention remains entirely on his father: "Is it the kind of compass where the top lifts up, like mine?' asks the boy eagerly, with eyes only for the man' (line 135).

An undercurrent of tension dominates the relationship between father and son and the author uses visual descriptions of their surroundings to create an ominous mood, the lake is a 'still black mirror' (line 159), 'ancient rocks glint like heaving carcasses asleep' (line 79), the wall is described as 'snaking' and the ponies are 'ghost-coloured' (line 145). Each have their own anxieties concerning loss and estrangement but their conversation revolves around inanimate objects: the tent, the compass and the torch; they do not discuss their fears. The boy uses these items to try and establish familiar ground with his father. On the compass, the boy tells his father: 'I keep mine by my bed', he then asks his father 'where do you keep yours?', the father replies: 'in my desk' (line 124). The mother's remark 'No hope of him relating to his son on any personal level (line 101)' reveals itself to be true as the story unfolds and despite the trip having presented an opportunity for the father to talk about feelings he fails to do so. His defeatist attitude becomes apparent as the story closes: 'In the plummeting darkness, the man's own anxiety began to mount. He could feel it gathering in the blackening chill: the aching certainty that already, only one year on from the separation, he has lost his son, his child' (line 167).

The final sentence suggests that the man and boy do become estranged because it indicates that this trip was a momentous one in both their memories, replaced by no more memories or trips:

Neither hears the horses moving round the tent in the night. For years to come, though, in his dreams the boy will see their wild fringed eyes and feel the deep thudding of their hooves.

From this we can assume that the father's fears constituted a self-fulfilling prophecy.

Part (b)

How does the writer present family life in **one** other story from *Sunlight on the Grass*.

In Aboulela's 'Something Old, Something New' we are given insights into two very different families from two very different cultures. The male protagonist is Scottish and his relationship with his parents is presented as more distant and reticent than that of the heroine's relationship with her Sudanese family. The presentation of family life in the story is one way in which Aboulela presents the cultural differences between the West and Islamic Sudan.

The Scotsman has dropped out of medical school and failed to fulfil the academic promise he had displayed at school, but his parents seem unconcerned by that: they are more worried about the type of life-style that he might fall into having dropped out:

Ever since he had dropped out of medical school, they had feared for his well-being, fretted that he would get sucked up into unemployment, drugs, depression; the underworld that throbbed and

dragged itself parallel to their active middle class life. (lines 173 –
176)

They 'struggled to hide their dismay' (lines 172 – 173) when they
learn of his conversion to Islam, but they are honest enough and
sufficiently concerned about their son to notice that he 'looked well'
(line 180), and seem to tolerate and love him, provided he avoids
talking about religion. When they meet his Sudanese girlfriend we
are told that 'the afternoon was a huge success' (line 191) and when
he announces that they intend to marry, 'there was a kind of relief in
his mother's eyes' (line 192). They want him to be settled and
happy, despite not understanding his conversion to Islam.

It would be easy to see the Scotsman's relationship with his family
as slightly distant and reticent: his parents do not seem to understand
his spiritual needs. But they clearly love him and care for him, and
they are welcoming and tolerant of his wife-to-be, although she
comes from a culture which is alien to them. Furthermore, he is still
in close contact with them; he takes his fiancée to meet them. One
can imagine some families where such a thing would be the cause of
a permanent estrangement.

The heroine's family is presented in a completely different way, and
live a life that is much more family-orientated and close-knit. When
he first sees her house, he notes that it is 'shabbier' (line 221) than
he had expected, but also 'larger'; it has to be larger because she has
five brothers and sisters and several nephews and nieces and an
uncle and aunt. She lives as part of a large extended family, whereas
it is implied that the Scotsman is an only child (Aboulela never
mentions any siblings). This leads to a realization on the Scotman's
behalf: 'She had always lived as part of a group, part of her [large]
family' (line 234) and that she had never had 'a desk of her own, a
room of her own, her own cupboard, her own dressing table, her own
mug' (lines 232 – 233) – not because of poverty, but because of the
sheer number of people who live in the house.

Aboulela seems to be suggesting (not that living as a large extended
family is inherently better) but that perhaps it is one reason why
cultural norms, habits and traditions are easier to maintain. During
the couple's courtship they are never alone because Sudanese culture
dictates that they should not be; the Scotsman pays a dowry for the
right to marry his bride; he does not see her without a headscarf until

after they are married; he would not be allowed to marry her were he not a Muslim; because of the uncle's death there is a set and ritualistic period of mourning during which the men have no contact whatsoever with the women; also, because of the protocols over mourning, special permission for the marriage has to be given by the bride's father or it could not take place. However, just as the Scotsman's parents showed tolerance to their daughter-in-law to be, none of the bride's family seem at all bothered by the fact she wants to marry a Scotsman – he is a Muslim and that is all that matters. This is a very different family tradition from the Scotsman's: he did not consult his parents before converting to Islam – which is an odd way of looking at it, but does demonstrate an important difference: we cannot imagine the heroine making such a major decision without involving her whole family.

And so Aboulela presents two families in 'Something Old, Something New' – one a modern, tolerant Western family who are perhaps a little distant from one another, but still full of love, care and concern; the other a large traditional Sudanese family, welcoming and tolerant, but perhaps a little claustrophobic to live amongst and very strict in their adherence to tradition.

Note

Family life is depicted in 'Anil' in a way that reflects the power structures of the village that Anil lives in and could have been used to answer part (b). 'When the Wasps Drowned' presents a family in an interesting way, because, although we meet the mother, there is no father mentioned, and the narrator and central character, Eveline, has to act as the surrogate mother to Therese and Tyler during the long summer holidays from school.

Question 11

Part (a)

How does the writer present Eveline in 'When the Wasps Drowned'?
Write about:

- what Eveline says and does

- the methods the writer uses to present Eveline

Wigfall uses Eveline as the narrator of 'When the Wasps Drowned' and in that sense she is presented very fully, as we see all the events from her point of view. In addition, Eveline appears to be narrating as in adult, looking back on what was a memorable for and momentous summer for her. What is interesting about the narrative style and language that Wigfall chooses to give Eveline as the narrator, is that at times she only hints at her feelings. Some readers have seen this as evidence that Eveline is in some ways sinister or deceitful about the events of that summer, but this essay will suggest a rather different interpretation.

It is a memorable summer for Eveline for a variety of reasons: she begins the story by telling us 'That was the summer Therese stepped on the wasps' nest and brought an end to our barefoot wanderings'; it is a long, hot summer of sunny days and no rain; on line 20 Eveline tells us 'That was the summer they dug up Mr Mordechai's garden' – although we are not told the reason until much later in the story. What Eveline leaves unsaid is that it is an important summer for in her development: we are never told her age, but it is clear that she is in her early teens and on the verge of adolescence. She is growing up and, although there are signs in the story that she is attracted to the adult world, the discovery of the young girl's corpse buried in the garden makes her fearful of the adult world.

In what ways is she attracted to the adult world? She tells us that that summer was 'the first time the garden walls seemed confining' (line 15), because she is old enough to see over them and she is aware of the 'tinny music of distant transistor radios' (lines 17 – 18); when she takes Therese and Tyler to the park she watches the boys who are gathered near the swings smoking; at home she sunbathes in a home-made bikini; she wears a ring that Therese has taken from the dead girl's hand; she uses the red dye from Smarties as pretend lipstick. Eveline tells us all these things but does not comment on them: she is clearly still a child but part of her hankers to be an adult.

In one sense she is an adult already because the children appear to live in a single-parent family, their mother works all day, and it is Eveline's responsibility to look after Therese and Tyler. She even cooks the evening meal when their mother returns from work. There is evidence that the family are not very well off: because of the extended heat-wave the swimming pool is very popular, but Eveline and her brother and sister are 'envious' (line 12) of the children waiting in the queue for the pool – which suggests, perhaps, that they cannot afford to use the swimming pool.

We are not told about any other characters' reactions to Eveline. She could be criticized, perhaps, because she does not play very actively with her brother and sister, but there is a big age gap and the extreme heat makes them all rather listless. She certainly reacts with shock when she hears Therese screaming because of the wasps and she runs from the kitchen to take swift action with the hosepipe to stop the wasps attacking her sister. She takes them to the park and, after the discovery of the dead girl, she listens with deep sympathy to Therese's nightmares and with a certain amount of envy to the comfort that their mother gives Therese: 'I wanted Mum's gentle shush in my own ear. When I closed my eyes I could see Therese's dream, the arm growing up through the soil' (lines 98 – 99) – which shows that despite her sense of confinement, she is still a child who needs comforting about their horrific discovery in the garden. Tellingly, although Eveline wears the ring – surely an act which shows a desire to enter the adult world – she is embarrassed by her actions and is careful to take it off before their mother returns from work.

The dead girl's arm is only discovered because Tyler has announced his intention to dig to Australia. Technically, Eveline should have reported the discovery of the body to the police and, at the end of the story, all three children say nothing when the police call and show them a photograph of a girl in a bikini just a few years older than Eveline herself. However, Eveline's decision to fill the hole back

109

with the earth that Tyler has dug out can be seen as a way of covering up something deeply frightening and disturbing, as an unwillingness to face up to the realities of the adult world that part of Eveline is so attracted to. The ending of the story may be ambivalent and inconclusive – but that is appropriate given Eveline's own feelings about growing up – a simultaneous attraction and dread of the adult world.

Part (b)

Write about how **one** other character is presented in **one** other story from *Sunlight on the Grass*.

The first thing we learn of Mrs Rutter in 'The Darkness Out There', is that 'She's a dear old thing, all on her own' (line 4). She has a 'wonky leg' and her home help is off with a bad back. These details initially evoke sympathy in the reader and from the description of the girl walking through the flowers, 'ox-eye daisies and vetch and cow parsley' (line 1), the reader is drawn into a false sense that all is well, everything is innocuous.

When the children meet Mrs Rutter, she initially seems to fit the description given of her: 'she seemed composed of circles, a cottage-loaf of a woman, with a face below which chins collapsed one into another, a creamy smiling pool of a face…' (line 96), however, the sentence continues: '…in which her eyes snapped and darted.' The description of her face and eyes immediately contradict one another and Lively uses this as a device to build tension, to make the reader question the woman's character. Similarly the description of the woman's innocently kitsch surroundings is contrasted with the smell of cabbage – something many children find repugnant. However, in this case the unpleasant details precede the inoffensive:

There was a smell of cabbage. The alcove by the fireplace was filled with china ornaments: big-eyed flop-eared rabbits and beribboned kittens and flowery milkmaids and a pair of naked chubby children wearing daisy chains. (line 101)

Still the reader is left with an undetermined opinion on the woman's character. She addresses the children affectionately calling them 'duck' and compliments Sandra on her prettiness, however, when Kerry mentions that he will soon be starting work at a local garage, clearly with some pride, Mrs Rutter verbally undermines his ambitions, saying: 'Well, I expect that's good steady money if you'd nothing special in mind' (line 113). This reveals a more callous side to the character and as the story progresses we learn that the woman is unable to identify the emotional impact of her words.

On line 123 Mrs Rutter broaches the subject of 'courting': 'You'll be courting before long yourself, I don't doubt. Like bees round the honeypot they'll be.' Sandra responds with embarrassment: 'The girl blushed. She looked at the floor...' (line 125). Mrs Rutter is obviously aware of the girl's imminent progression into adulthood and despite this on line 141 she invites Sandra to lift her skirt up, ostensibly to avoid getting it dirty. This introduces a more sinister side to the character, her motives left unclear: 'Mind your pretty skirt, pull it up a bit, there's only me to see if you're showing a bit of bum.' On line 152 Mrs Rutter continues to pursue the theme of boyfriends: 'I expect you've got lots of boyfriends, though, haven't you?' Sandra's response again indicates discomfort: 'The girl poked in a crack at a clump of fluff.' The writer tacitly builds a picture of a woman insensitive to the emotions of those around her and certainly a character not in tune with adolescent psychology.

When Mrs Rutter recounts the story of the German plane crash her insensitivity is made concrete. She blunders through the story, unaware of the children's mounting horror and despite professing to like children several times and lamenting her own childlessness she reveals that the injured airman was in his early twenties (line 323), not much older than Kerry himself. Her inhumanity becomes sealed when she reveals that she took souvenirs from the fallen plane and in her final words to the children the conflict between her self-perception and her actions on the night of the crash reveal a deeply entrenched hypocrisy: 'I like having someone young about the place, once in a while. I've got sympathy with young people...' (line342).

Lively closes the story with the children's responses and their strong sense of morality further amplifies Mrs Rutter's immorality. Kerry shakes with clenched fists (line 353) while Sandra reveals that her innocence has been lost through the exchange with Mrs Rutter:

One moment you were walking in long grass with the sun on your hair and birds singing and the next you glimpsed darkness, an inescapable darkness. The darkness was out there and it was a part of you and you would never be without it, ever.

She walked behind him, through a world grown unreliable, in which flowers sparkle and birds sing but everything is not as it appears, oh no.

In real time the reader learns, alongside the children, that characters are not necessarily as they initially appear to be and as the time spent with Mrs Rutter strips back the layers of her character, a more sinister, inhumane person is laid bare.

Note

Other stories that would have been good to use in answer to part (b) are 'My Polish Teacher's Tie', focusing on the presentation of Carla or 'On Seeing the 100% Perfect Girl One Beautiful April Morning' because the narrator is presented so clearly through his own narration.

Question 12

Part (a)

How do you respond to the ending of 'When the Wasps Drowned' and how does Wigfall make you respond as you do by the ways she writes?

The very ending of 'When the Wasps Drowned' produces a very unusual response and is worth quoting at length. The police have just visited the house and shown Eveline and her brother and sister a photo of a missing girl – whom we assume is the girl whose dead body the children have found while Tyler was digging to Australia. In the photograph the girl seems only slightly older than Eveline. The children deny any knowledge of the girl and Wigfall ends the story with this paragraph:

I shut the door and we waited a while, heard them walking down our garden path and unlatching Mr Mordechai's gate next door. My fingers, fiddling unconsciously, played with the ring for a moment as we stood together in the dark hallway. None of us said a thing. Taking Therese and Tyler by the hand, I turned, and we stepped back out into the sunlight of the garden. (lines 125 – 129)

We think that this ending is positive and comforting: it is crucial that the whole story is narrated by Eveline, and how we react to the end may well depend on how we react to Eveline herself. For us the final sentence displays care and protection (Eveline takes Therese and Tyler by the hand) and she leads them into the innocence of the sunlight of the garden, where they can continue to be children, untroubled by the dangers of the adult world.

Of course, it could be argued that Eveline is deliberately not facing up to the truth, just as she had told Tyler to fill in the hole where the dead girl's arm was buried, and then told no one about their horrific discovery. This is certainly true: technically Eveline has committed a crime by not reporting their discovery of the dead girl's body, but her reasons for not doing so are very much to do, it could be argued, with her age, her own attraction to and yet horror of the adult world, and a desire to preserve her own childish innocence for just a little while longer. After all, Eveline is still a child and although she plays at being an adult because she is on the cusp of adolescence, the adult world remains a very frightening and intimidating place. She asks Tyler to fill in the whole that he was digging to Australia, not because she wishes to conceal a crime, but because the reality of the dead girl is too frightening and dreadful for her to contemplate.

It can also be argued with some justification that the ending of the story is slightly inconclusive in that we don't know exactly what happens. However, we do know what happens in the wake of the police visit to the children: the police proceed to dig Mr Mordechai's garden up, presumably in an effort to find the corpse of the dead girl – we are warned that this will happen in line 20 of the story. But who buried the girl and who murdered her, her identity and the exact circumstances of her death remain mysteries. We have no idea whether Mr Mordechai is involved in what has happened to the girl.

However, we would argue that this is entirely deliberate on Wigfall's part, and part of her presentation of Eveline who is, after all, the narrator of the story. Eveline is genuinely frightened and disturbed by the discovery of the dead girl, and it is as though she ends her narrative on a positive note, because she wants to erase the memory from her mind – and, therefore, feels no need and no desire to pass on to the reader any of the details concerning the girl – her identity, her murderer's identity and so on. For Eveline it is much better psychologically for her to end her narrative by leading her younger brother and sister out into the sunny, innocent garden of their childhood.

Part (b)

How do you respond to the ending of **one** other story from *Sunlight on the Grass* and how do the writer's methods make you respond as you do?

The ending of 'Compass and Torch' reveals the mother's words on line 101 as a proleptic irony: 'No hope of him relating to his son on any personal, day-to-day level! No hope of him trying to RELATE to him, full stop!' By the conclusion of this story father and son have discussed nothing on an emotional level, they have both internalized their fears and conversation has revolved around the inanimate objects of the compass and torch.

Despite the child's obvious devotion to his father and the father's reciprocal adoration, the ending seems sadly inevitable. We learn that the father is on the cusp of giving up: He could feel it in the blackening chill: the aching certainty that already, only one year on from the separation, he has lost his son, his child' (line 168). The past tense use of 'lost' as opposed to 'losing' is also indicative of the relationship's conclusion; the father appears to have reconciled himself to this notion. This is frustrating as a reader because through the omniscient narrative we are party to the information which would stop this estrangement, namely the mutual adoration between father and son.

In the final section of the story, beginning on line 161, the writer refers to the assorted camping paraphernalia with repeated use of the word 'their': 'They have pitched their tent, they have lit their stove, and in the quick-dropping dark at the foot of the mountain they have eaten their reconstituted soup.' This reinforces the connection between father and son and, as a reader, makes us want this unit or relationship to work all the more.

On line 165 Baines refers to the gas canister: '…the man failed to light it first time and the flare sputtered and died.' This detail could be seen to represent a portent; the flare is the relationship. Will it too 'sputter and die'?

While we are not actually told that the father and son become estranged, the final sentences suggest that this was a seminal event in both lives:

Neither hears the horses moving round the tent in the night.

For years to come, though, in his dreams the boy will see their wild fringed eyes and feel the deep thudding of their hooves (lines 173-175).

This, together with the reference to 'plummeting darkness' (line 166) and 'blackening chill' (line 167), creates the impression that the outcome for the relationship is bleak and the father's ability to 'blank out pain' (line 172) indicates that he does not have the impetus or drive to sustain their relationship.

Note

The ending of 'Anil' with its use of a single sentence which returns the focus of the story to Marimuthu, the headman's brother, is an interesting way to end the story because it reminds us of the corrupt way the village is run and the cover up of a murder. More widely, the ending of 'Anil' is revelatory because Noor presents Ragunathan, Anil's father, as keenly aware of the power the headman has over him as well as the moral dilemma involved in accepting a good, private education for his only son in return for covering up a murder. Kerry's final remark in 'The Darkness Out There' – 'It makes you want to throw up… someone like that' (line 360) is an important reflection of the horrific revelations about the past in the story. The narrator's confident assertion at the end of 'On Seeing the 100% Perfect Girl One Beautiful April Morning' – 'Yes, that's it, that is what I should have said to her' (line 117) – demonstrates his slightly delusional fantasy and highlights the fairy story element of the story.

CPSIA information can be obtained at www.ICGtesting.com
Printed in the USA
LVOW05s1558181114

414313LV00002B/485/P